Salmi
a quattro chori

RECENT RESEARCHES IN MUSIC

A-R Editions publishes seven series of critical editions, spanning the history of Western music, American music, and oral traditions.

RECENT RESEARCHES IN THE MUSIC OF THE MIDDLE AGES
AND EARLY RENAISSANCE
    Charles M. Atkinson, general editor

RECENT RESEARCHES IN THE MUSIC OF THE RENAISSANCE
    James Haar, general editor

RECENT RESEARCHES IN THE MUSIC OF THE BAROQUE ERA
    Christoph Wolff, general editor

RECENT RESEARCHES IN THE MUSIC OF THE CLASSICAL ERA
    Eugene K. Wolf, general editor

RECENT RESEARCHES IN THE MUSIC OF THE NINETEENTH
AND EARLY TWENTIETH CENTURIES
    Rufus Hallmark, general editor

RECENT RESEARCHES IN AMERICAN MUSIC
    John M. Graziano, general editor

RECENT RESEARCHES IN THE ORAL TRADITIONS OF MUSIC
    Philip V. Bohlman, general editor

Each edition in *Recent Researches* is devoted to works by a single composer or to a single genre. The content is chosen for its high quality and historical importance, and each edition includes a substantial introduction and critical report. The music is engraved according to the highest standards of production using our own proprietary software called MusE.

For information on establishing a standing order to any of our series, or for editorial guidelines on submitting proposals, please contact:

A-R Editions, Inc.
801 Deming Way
Madison, Wisconsin 53717

800 736-0070 (U.S. book orders)
608 836-9000 (phone)
608 831-8200 (fax)
http://www.areditions.com

Lodovico Grossi da Viadana

Salmi a quattro chori

Edited by Gerhard Wielakker

A-R Editions, Inc.
Madison

A-R Editions, Inc., Madison, Wisconsin 53717
© 1998 by A-R Editions, Inc.

A-R Editions is pleased to support scholars and performers
in their use of *Recent Researches* material for study or performance. Subscribers to any of the *Recent Researches* series,
as well as patrons of subscribing institutions, are invited to
apply for information about our "Copyright Sharing
Policy."

Printed in the United States of America

ISBN 0-89579-398-9
ISSN 0484-0828

⊚ The paper used in this publication meets the minimum
requirements of the American National Standard for
Information Sciences—Permanence of Paper for Printed
Library Materials, ANSI Z39.48-1984.

Contents

Acknowledgments vi

Introduction vii
  Church Music at the Beginning of the Seventeenth Century vii
  Vespers viii
  Viadana's Vespers x
  The Score xi
  Practices of Variable Forces ad Libitum xiii
  Notes xvi

Texts and Translations xix

Plates xxiv

Salmi a quattro chori
  Modo di concertare i detti salmi a quattro chori 2
      I. Deus in adjutorium 5
     II. Dixit Dominus (Psalm 109) 11
    III. Confitebor tibi (Psalm 110) 27
     IV. Beatus vir (Psalm 111) 44
      V. Laudate pueri (Psalm 112) 57
     VI. Laudate Dominum (Psalm 116) 71
    VII. Laetatus sum (Psalm 121) 82
   VIII. Nisi Dominus (Psalm 126) 98
     IX. Lauda Jerusalem (Psalm 147) 112
      X. Magnificat 130
    XIa. Sinfonia a doi tenori 153
    XIb. Magnificat 155

Critical Report 175
  Source 175
  Editorial Methods 175
  Critical Notes 176

Acknowledgments

The editor would like to thank the many friends and colleagues who have helped him in the preparatory work for this edition, and most especially the following: Dr. Leo Plenckers (Department of Musicology, University of Amsterdam), for his highly useful advice in general; Dr. Frans Wiering, whose musicological expertise proved highly valuable; Norbert Bartelsman, for his professional advice concerning the thorough-bass; and Dr. Mario Armellini of the Civico Museo Bibliografico Musicale of Bologna, for making the source available. The work of Mrs. Mary Adams in assisting the editor with the English of the Introduction, Critical Report, and the translations of the psalm texts was also invaluable.

Introduction

In 1612 the publisher Giacomo Vincenti of Venice printed the *Salmi a quattro chori* by Lodovico Grossi da Viadana. The famous preface ("Modo di concertare") to these psalms is quoted regularly because it provides not only, for the first time in history, instructions for the director, but various other directions as well, thus furnishing important details on performance practice of around 1600.[1]

This opus comprises the ingredients for a complete Vespers. After the Mass, Vespers was the most "popular" service in the religious life of the people. Whereas Renaissance composers contributed to this tradition with polyphonic settings of only the hymn and the Magnificat, the last quarter of the sixteenth century saw an enormous output of polyphonic psalm publications. Most of these were composed using *falsobordone* technique, in which psalm verses were set with simple syllabic declamation on one chord leading to a short cadence in the mode of the plainsong psalm verses with which they were sung in alternation (*alternatim*). While melodically richer settings of the polyphonic verses were also written, the alternation with plainsong verses generally remained the rule.[2]

Around 1600 the character of psalm collections changed by becoming more concentrated in content. Instead of stringing together dozens of psalms for the whole church year, only the most common requirements of the liturgical calendar were set (many psalms were appropriate to more than one category of feasts). Thus a very specific framework for the important feast days came into being, of which this Vespers by Viadana is a beautiful example. This change was partly a result of the larger shift in compositional style that took place around 1600. With the appearance of basso continuo and the concertante style of solo and ensemble combinations of vocal and instrumental voices, the baroque idiom had arrived. This posed serious problems for psalm composers in general and for composers of polychoral psalm settings in particular. That a pragmatist such as Viadana could come up with ingenious solutions to the musical problems of his time had already been proven with his *Cento concerti ecclesiastici* (1602), as a result of which he would go down in history as the "inventor of basso continuo."[3] With the conception of his *Salmi a quattro chori* he again offered his contemporaries practical assistance, this time with the problems that had arisen in polychoral psalm music. But he achieved this end in such a lively and original style and with such musical eloquence that the work truly stands as an artistically as well as a historically valuable document.

What in fact did Viadana achieve in his Vespers? To come up with a good answer to this question, it will be useful first to describe the development of church music in the early seventeenth century, especially in connection with the above-mentioned problems for composers of polychoral psalm music. Next, the social and liturgical background of Vespers will be considered. Only then can the composition itself and Viadana's historic role be properly understood in context.

Church Music at the Beginning of the Seventeenth Century

Small-scale Works

The impressive *cori spezzati* style gave way in most northern Italian cities to the rapidly emerging small-scale concertato motet: music for a small body of soloists and continuo. In these works, solo singers and violinists poured out expressive and flexible melodies, regrouping in the course of the piece, and possibly coming together in ripieni. The melodies were not superficial—on the contrary, their expressiveness was often deeply rooted in the text. Thus emerged solo motets in delicate duos, trios, and quartets; even five- and six-part settings were transparent in texture because of their soloistic character and the frequent treatment of the voices in pairs or groups.

This genre was quickly made fashionable by men such as Alessandro Grandi, one of the most gifted composers of church music in his time, the progressive Giovanni Francesco Capello, and many others. They achieved the artistic development and sublimation of the settings for which Viadana, out of practical necessity, had laid the foundation with his *Cento concerti ecclesiastici*. A generation later the brilliant Giovanni Antonio Rigatti was to excel above all others in the small-scale motet.

This new concertato style posed huge problems for composers of psalm settings. Psalm texts were felt to be neutral and therefore suited to polyphonic or homophonic settings in the *stile antico*, not to the affective approach to text of the new style. *Falsobordone* was regarded as an old-fashioned technique and new *alternatim* schemes were rejected because the modern idiom was irreconcilable with plainsong. Stefano Bernardi composed psalms that set off short solos and duets against contrasting tutti sections. Francesco Bellazzi employed a genuine concertato idiom with instrumental interpolations. But they could not eliminate the impression of a sort of forced marriage, because the long stretches of text could not be developed expressively.

Large-scale Works

The demand for small-scale solo motets was further magnified by a non-musical factor. Inflation and the petty wars of the city fathers brought an economic malaise that resulted in a drastic reduction of choirs. In many small provincial towns the new style was welcomed out of financial necessity because they could no longer afford to maintain polychoral practices.

But there was also a musical factor that made the *cori spezzati* unsuitable for the new baroque idiom: the preconceived arrangement of fixed groups seemed too rigid a starting point for an affective treatment of text and for soloistic expressiveness. No one was more aware of this than Giovanni Gabrieli himself. In his later music he states how a more individual approach to the text is realized through a style that might be called "variable concertato": music in which scoring, texture, and grouping vary continually in the course of the work and are no longer decided beforehand. His motet *In ecclesiis* is a superb example of this. Many composers, including Amadio Freddi and the versatile Grandi, based their large-scale motets on this variable style.

Seen in this light, the problems facing composers wishing to write Vespers psalms in the *cori spezzati* style become clear. This pompous style with its fixed choral blocks was not sufficiently supple to be molded according to the texts in the modern manner; the long, neutral texts themselves also deterred an individual mood expression. In addition, formal problems arose out of the large structures. Valerio Bona and Antonio Mortaro wrote psalms in the grand style of Gabrieli but did not manage to avoid, among other things, long *falsobordone* passages of the lengthy texts. Later, in 1623, Ignazio Donati was to take the concertato style to its utmost limits, as it were, in his fascinating *Salmi boscarecci*.[4] This is multi-functional music that is provided with such a range of possibilities of scoring that its style might be called "mixed concertato."

Variable concertato, mixed concertato—but how to give the right variety to the grand style? Who could bring concertato elements into solemn psalm settings in such a way that one could speak of something like "grand concertato style?" The answers to both these questions lie in Viadana's Vespers, his *Salmi a quattro chori*, presented here. Before moving on to that specific work, however, a more general consideration of Vespers as a socioreligious observance is in order.

Vespers

Social Background

A very old tradition, which persisted well into the twentieth century all over Europe, required that on Sundays and feast days the faithful should attend Vespers, one of the most important compulsory services of the Divine Office.[5] The enormous increase in the production of Vespers music around 1600 reflected the huge growth of this custom in the whole of northern Italy.

Not only religious motives were involved; it was also a reflection of the political and economic status of a city. Around 1600 there were as yet no opera houses, and city-dwellers could only listen to music in church. The city councils therefore had an interest in good church music, for it consolidated the prestige of the city. The Mass and Vespers were closely interwoven with city life.

In many cities, in addition to the churches, the so-called fraternities were still in operation, charitable institutions which cared for the poor, the sick, and the orphaned. These had their own churches and services, with professional choirs often under excellent direction. Furthermore, churches often made contracts with fraternities, regulating the hire of one another's musicians. First-rate musicians (including Giovanni Gabrieli and Giovanni Croce) appeared on the salary lists of the fraternities.

Thus on feast days splendid ad hoc ensembles were assembled which helped turn Mass and Vespers into impressive events. Often this was coupled with processions outside the church buildings: colorful pageants with sumptuously attired prelates, canons, and civic dignitaries. Arrayed with banners, flags, candles, and relics, they processed through the streets, singing and playing, creating a theatrical entertainment every citizen could admire. In short, they were imposing manifestations of religious and civic power.

It was naturally the rich cities that were able to transform such days into real "events," and equally naturally it was Venice, the city that had made a principle of impressing and astonishing visitors, that was to lead the way. In Venice a fraternity was called a *Scuola Grande*, of which the city had no less than six. The *Scuola Grande di San Rocco* was the best known, and it was precisely the effect the city intended which the travelling Englishman Thomas Coryat experienced at the festivities on the feast day of Saint Rocco: he was "rapt up with Saint Paul into the third heaven" during a Vespers in 1608 that lasted for hours.[6]

Of course, other cities also had very active fraternities. In Ferrara there were two, the *Accademia della Morte* and the *Accademia dello Spirito Santo*. In Parma the fraternity was called the *Compagnia della Steccata*, and it is of particular interest for the present discussion because of the light it shed on the relative importance accorded Mass and Vespers. The fraternity held the Blessed Virgin in special veneration and a Mass was sung in her honor every Sunday. All Marian feast days were celebrated with solemn Mass and Vespers. The festivities around the feast of the Annunciation began on the previous day with a public proclamation by the city pipers and evening Vespers (First Vespers). On the day itself, for Mass and Second Vespers, the fraternity augmented the choir with musicians from the cathedral and the ducal chapel (the court chapel of the Farneses), and players accompanied the singers during the procession, which included secular princes and their retinues. From the statutes of the *Compagnia della Steccata*, it seems that the emphasis lay far more on the Office than on the Mass: Mass was celebrated ceremoniously with figural music about five times a year, Vespers more than twenty times. All of this shows us that, alongside the Mass, Vespers held a very important place within religious activities, and that these in turn were very closely interwoven with the day-to-day life of the people.

Liturgical Background

The fixed elements (Ordinary) of Vespers are as follows: *Deus in adjutorium*, Magnificat, *Pater noster,* closing formula. The changing elements (Proper) are: antiphons, *capitulum, responsorium breve, oratorio, commemoratio.* The five psalms occupy a position somewhere in between these two categories. The first three psalms are almost always Psalms 109, 110, and 111, often with Psalm 112 as the fourth (Vulgate numbering). Thus it is often the differentiation of the last two psalms that distinguishes the Vespers of various feasts from one another.

On the basis of Viadana's psalm settings we can, as it were, see "retrospectively" at which feasts his Vespers could have been sung. Of the feasts still known today those are, in the *Proprium de tempore:* Christmas (I), the Circumcision (I–II), Epiphany (I), Ascension (I–II), Pentecost (I), Trinity Sunday (I), and All Saints (I).[7] Basically all of the numerous saints' days are eligible, for in the case of the male saints Viadana's psalms in the First Vespers for both the *Proprium Sanctorum* and the *Commune Sanctorum* are appropriate: Psalms 109, 110, 111, 112, and 116.[8] For the female saints the same five psalms from the *Proprium* and the *Commune* are always sung in both Vespers: Psalms 109, 112, 121, 126, and 147. Here of course the Marian feasts predominate, of which fifteen were at that time already very well known.[9]

If feast days thus have a number of psalms in common, the antiphons, as songs belonging to the Proper of Vespers, are always different. In plainsong Vespers the psalms and Magnificat were always sung in the mode in which the antiphon was sung. But in polyphonic Vespers the modes of the psalms are fixed. From the plainsong books it appears that in the entire church year there is not a single feast for which the mode of the antiphon corresponds to the modes of Viadana's psalms. Even if by chance such a feast should be found it would prove nothing, since this Vespers is intended for the entire church year.

We now know, partly from the study by Stephen Bonta,[10] that the explanation for this situation lies in the fact that both in plainsong and polyphonic Vespers the plainsong antiphons were replaced by instrumental pieces.[11] In Adriano Banchieri's *L'Organo suonarino* this practice is described in detail.[12] Here Banchieri gives precise instructions concerning the rules to be followed by the organist during Vespers. In addition to the instrumental substitutes for the antiphons, he also mentions preludes, postludes, and interludes. There are also rules regarding genre, mode, and duration. Thus Banchieri states *where, what, how,* and *how long* the organist must play. He also provides pieces. In *L'Organo suonarino* we find included, among other things, a set of "five sonatas printed in score and appended for use with the five psalms that are normally sung at Vespers," as Banchieri states;[13] in addition there is an *Ingresso d'un Ripieno,* to be played before Vespers; various *Capricii,* to be played instead of the Magnificat antiphon; and a *Ripieno per il Deo Gratias,* to be played after the *Deo gratias.* Banchieri's instructions are intended for plainsong Vespers in monasteries and small parishes. But for polyphonic Vespers the role of the organ is taken over by instrumental ensembles.[14] In the cathedrals of the larger cities, Vespers on major feast days meant a splendid, lengthy feast that was a musical and liturgical reflection of the social life discussed above.[15]

From Banchieri's precise classification according to the eight modes we can see that the "organ antiphon" had to be played in the same mode as the subsequent psalm or Magnificat: the organist had to maintain modal unity with the plainsong. In polyphonic Vespers there is less emphasis on this requirement. In festive polyphonic Vespers the *when* and *what* remain important, but the *how* (mode) and *how long* were less relevant, so that the director had a certain freedom in the structuring of his "Vespers program." The rule of thumb was, roughly speaking, that the director chose the instrumental interludes *unless* the composer himself provided compositions written specifically for the purpose. Claudio Monteverdi was primarily interested not in instrumental music but in the problems generated by the combination of words and music. Therefore in his Marian Vespers the antiphonal interludes have a significant vocal input and are composed by Monteverdi himself; the director may choose an instrumental substitute for the missing Magnificat antiphon, in this case preferably a polychoral canzona.[16] With Viadana the situation is reversed: he writes a "Sinfonia a doi tenori" just before the second Magnificat, while the other pieces, and also the hymn, are optional.[17]

These pieces were regarded as much as providing welcome musical relief as following liturgical rule. This is proven by Viadana's Compline for double choir.[18] The Compline comprises only three psalms (Psalms 4, 90, and 133, sung directly one after another) framed by just one antiphon. Nonetheless Viadana gives the organist the option of playing a "concerto" after Psalm 4, and even a sort of intermezzo in the middle of Psalm 90.[19]

It was not uncommon for two Magnificats to be set in a Vespers collection, one a sober setting, the other richer. One or the other could be chosen, probably based on the effect sought in a First or Second Vespers and on the musicians available. In Viadana's Vespers, the first Magnificat is obviously the simpler one, while the second is much more impressive, a tour de force of expressive musical effects often conveyed in virtuosic solo passages. This would indicate that the second Magnificat was intended to be sung at First Vespers.

Viadana makes reference to the plainsong tradition of psalm settings by deriving the openings of his psalms from Gregorian intonations. Beyond that, at the beginning of Psalm 121 (mm. 1–6), the tenor recalls the old cantus firmus technique by singing the first plainsong half verse, and in the *Gloria Patri* of Psalm 112 (mm. 86–92), the quinto sings a complete psalm verse on the so-called *Tonus Peregrinus*. But perhaps the most impressive reference to plainsong occurs in the alleluia of the *Deus in adjutorium:* from measure 9, the lowest parts of all choirs sing, in cantus-firmus style, the well-known *Alleluia Dies sanctificatus* from the Mass repertory (see the *Liber Usualis,* 409). Here Viadana notes the vocal parts (though not the instrumental parts) in ligatures, making apparent to eye as well as ear the ultimate source for his polyphonic Vespers.

Viadana's Vespers

As has been noted, composers of polychoral music found it difficult to reconcile the "neutral" character of psalm texts with the greater expressive demands of the modern style in a way that created the sense of an overall structural conception. Girolamo Giacobbi took a step toward solving this problem when he introduced a new element in the second Magnificat of his psalm collection of 1609.[20] While the psalms and first Magnificat were set for two choirs (a low choir and a SATB choir), the second Magnificat was set for five: two low choirs, a high choir, a SATB choir, and a fifth choir consisting of a solo soprano and bass. What was innovative was the fifth choir, for with the inclusion of a "two-part solo choir" separated from the other choirs, Giacobbi introduced a concertato element into the polychoral style.

Giacobbi's cue placed Viadana in a position by and large to solve the abovementioned stylistic problem both musically and practically. In his four-choir conception, Choir I is for five soloists, expanding on Giacobbi's two-soloist concertato group, while Choir II is the main SATB *capella* group. Both these choirs are essential to the work and lie at the heart of the musical solution of bringing the expressive capabilities of a solo ensemble into contrast with a full choir. Choirs III and IV, however, both in four parts, are treated as ripieno groups that could be dispensed with if necessary. This was a totally new idea that only became general practice by around 1630. Conversely, the high and low ripieno groups could not only be retained but be doubled, as could Choir II. Viadana mentioned these options in his preface. Thus at one stroke he provided the practical solution: rich cities with cathedral status could perform this Vespers in a version for four to seven choirs; smaller cities, plagued by economic problems, could make do with the basic complement of Choirs I and II, who conduct the real musical dialogue.

Viadana's approach was to make its influence felt throughout Europe, especially in Germany, then on the threshold of the horrors of the Thirty Years' War. This conflict would eventually cause a drastic reduction in recruitment for Heinrich Schütz's *Kapelle* in Dresden. In the small-scale concertato style which Schütz was then forced to adopt, he took up the innovations made by Grandi in this area.[21] But in the *spezzato* style he made from the outset grateful use of the model of which he was to become so fond: the modern concept, created by Viadana, of only a few "compulsory" choirs, with *Complementchöre* to be added freely for purely spatial effect.

The purely musical advances Viadana made were also very influential. He strictly divided the sections, as a result of which the massive tutti sections are clearly differentiated from the solo episodes, written in modern polyphony. This brings us to one of Viadana's most important achievements: the tremendous emancipation of the five-part solo choir. Other composers (including Giacobbi in the psalms and first Magnificat of his 1609 collection) drew their soloists from the full choirs and were therefore not yet in a position to have a real concertato dialogue between a solo group and those choirs; even in the second Magnificat alluded to above, Giacobbi did not fully realize the musical potential for contrast between his two-part solo choir and the other four full choirs. Not for nothing, therefore, does Viadana emphasize in his preface that "everything depends on the good and modern singing of the soloists," since his Vespers has a real "primo choro concertato," a *choro favorito.* The addition of choir voices to this solo group would destroy the contrast, but here this is made totally impossible in any case by the very advanced style in which the soloists sing their virtuoso verse sections, embellished with rhythmically capricious ornaments and fast runs, and manifesting a rich diversity in their constantly changing voice combinations.

Another highly essential innovation is the intrusion of dialogue between this purely solo group, which mostly has the initiative, and the other groups, which have a more responsive function (although they sometimes take the initiative themselves or interrupt suddenly). In this way a very lively interactive process is set in motion, with the groups usually finding resolution immediately after one another, often syncopated within the beat, with the help of the declamatory anacrusis. Anyone who hears the success with which this is worked out will realize what a magnificent foreshadowing of what lay ahead takes place: that of the interaction between soloist and orchestra as in a Mozart piano concerto. Here, in 1612, we have one of the first and clearest anticipations of the later concerto style!

This Vespers is also lent particular eloquence by Viadana's inward responsiveness to the text, which he puts forward again and again in a most distinctive manner by depicting it with great flexibility, using constantly changing musical means. In Psalm 111 at *dispersit* (dispersed) the canto and alto soloists sing rhythmically in opposition to one another. In Psalm 147 the word *velociter* (swiftly) is tossed to and fro between the two main choirs; a fine drizzle of "pointilistically" scattered fast notes descends at *nebulam sicut cinerem spargit* (he scattereth the hoarfrost like ashes); runs of eighth and sixteenth notes sparkle as though sprinkled from a vaporizer at *flabit spiritus* (he causeth the wind to blow); and dazzling melismas gush forth at *fluent aquae* (the waters flow). In the two Magnificats powerful homophonic tutti pillars rise up at *omnes generationes* (all generations) while at *humiles* (them of low degree) the homophony is briefly and simply stated between melismatic passages. On a deeper psychological level, in a passage such as *Et misericordia* (And his mercy) of the second Magnificat, the charity of the God-fearing is reproduced. Bitter-sweet chromaticism and striking intervals conjure up a particular atmosphere that is more than word-painting: through his profound ability to identify with the text, Viadana evokes its mood throughout an entire section. This is the modern, affective approach to the text of which I spoke above.

The text of the "Sinfonia a doi tenori" is an original creation, clearly inspired by the song of Miriam, the sister of Moses and Aaron (along with Deborah, she was one of the illustrious singers mentioned in the Old Testament). Her song addresses the Lord after crossing the dry ground of the Red Sea (see Exodus 15:20–21), and it actually repeats (in the manner of a refrain) the beginning of the song sung by Moses and the Israelites (Exodus 15:1). This is interesting to point out in the present context of Viadana's polychoral Vespers, as Miriam in effect leads the women in responding to the men. In any case, the fact that in the text of the "Sinfonia a doi tenori," Mary is cast as a musician is highly exceptional. Obviously the poet has transferred the imagery of Miriam the musician to Mary, so that she, too, becomes a *timpanistria*, playing the tambourine. The parallel drawn between the shorter texts of Miriam's song and the "Sinfonia" suggests a further parallel between the longer texts, and in fact there are similarities between Moses' hymn of praise (Exodus 15:1–18) and the Magnificat.

The score is also interesting in terms of harmony. Through continuous shifts from major to minor, tension is maintained constantly in the musical conversation, all the more since these harmonic shifts often coincide with the moments at which the groups themselves suddenly alternate. And while formerly *falsobordone* was a device used as a matter of course by many composers when setting lengthy texts, to Viadana it became an instrument, one of many features of his style to be integrated into an overall concept. He puts the older technique to use in tutti passages, for instance, in the impressive opening (*Domine ad adjuvandum*) and in the concluding doxology of the psalms (*Gloria Patri / Sicut erat*).

Finally, the instrumental timbres of organ, harpsichord, chitarrone, strings, cornett, and trombone must be mentioned, which augment the contrasts between the high and low ripieno choirs. These lend the composition the splendid coloring that similarly attracts us so much to the paintings of an artist such as Tintoretto. Thus the fascinating, kaleidoscopic shadings of Viadana's score are unfolded in all their glory and splendor: an imposing tableau of radiance, movement, and contrast, whose penetrating eloquence still speaks to us undiminished in the twentieth century.

The Score

Notes on the Vocal Parts

The solo *choro favorito* leads the real musical dialogue with the *capella*, which has more than one voice to a part. The two ripieno choirs never sing without this *capella*, and therefore they can be dispensed with if need be. Economic necessity sometimes forced the director to use minimal forces, but it is obvious that the omission of Choirs III and IV causes an enormous attenuation. For in this way much of the spatial effect is lost, and "space" is a real "instrument" in the acoustical game of polychoral music. Furthermore, the element of contrast provided by the ripieno choirs is essential: a high, bright Choir III versus a low, dark-sounding Choir IV, the chiaroscuro effect being further intensified by the shading of the instruments. The omission of the ripieno choirs would destroy all these nuances of timbre, leaving a meagre result (perhaps, speaking in terms of the comparison drawn above, a black-and-white reproduction of a Tintoretto painting).

In Viadana's time alto parts were exclusively sung by falsetto men's voices. The only question is whether the canto part of Choir I was not also intended for a man's voice (falsetto or castrato) instead of a boy's voice. In the preface of his *Cento concerti ecclesiastici*, composed within the same framework as that of the *choro favorito* here, Viadana expresses his preference for men's voices over boy sopranos in solo settings.[22]

The quinto voice of the *choro favorito* normally sings in the range of a tenor. However, in four passages, the quinto is paired in a duet with and made to match the range of a voice other than tenor. For instance, in Psalm 111, measures 50–62, the quinto voice sings in the range of a bass in a duet with the basso soloist. Practically, of course, this means that a second basso soloist is required to sing the quinto part. In Psalm 112, measures 1–10, it is another canto that is required as the quinto sings in the soprano range in a duet with the first canto soloist. Two other passages, both in the second Magnificat (see mm. 1–22 and 113–20), also require a second canto to sing with the first. (Although at m. 113 the source does state that the quinto is to be sung by a "Canto ò Tenore," indicating the possibility that the tenor of the *choro favorito* could sing the line an octave lower than notated.) In short, the need of another basso soloist and another canto soloist means that instead of five soloists in the *choro favorito*, seven are required. Furthermore, yet another "hidden" canto is called upon in the passage of the second Magnificat (mm. 121–36) where a soprano is instructed to sing from behind a screen (the instruction reads "Basso solo è Soprano da nascosto"). Concealing the soprano in this way was not new but was based on experiments of this sort by Donati.[23]

As Oliver Strunk notes, with the term *à voci pari* for Choir IV (see preface) "Viadana follows the usual practice of his time," which applies this expression "not only to music in a single register, high or low, but also to music in which the over-all register is relatively restricted."[24]

Instruments and Voices

Michael Praetorius, in his *Syntagma musicum,* volume III,[25] gives a comprehensive description of instrumental practices in the early seventeenth century. The composer, says Praetorius, has a particular family of instruments in mind, which we can recognize from the *claves signatae,* the characteristic clefs of a choir.[26] Thus a choir in which the highest clefs consist of G2–C1–C2 is pre-eminently suited to cornetts. These "cornett clefs" were in Viadana's time very often used for the *choro acuto,* although Choir III in this Vespers has C1–C1–C3–C4. The cornetts may be replaced by or combined with violins.[27] In the low register one has the *claves signatae* that typify trombone or bassoon choirs: C3–C4–C4–F3, C3–C4–F3–F4, or C4–F3–F4–F5. Such combinations belong to the *choro grave,* and Viadana uses the middle combination for his Choir IV. In this group gambas may replace the wind instruments, but the dark, sonorous color of bassoons and above all trombones is here characteristic. Of the stringed instruments, both the gamba family and that of the viola da braccio had a very large ambit. This was also the case with transverse flutes and recorders. These families were known in all sorts of sizes and covered the entire range of the human voice. Their *claves signatae* (C1–C3–C4–F4 or C2–C3–C4–F4) were especially characteristic because they related to the voice parts of the *chorus vocalis* in polychoral works. Thus the term "Capella" was added to indicate that here all parts must be sung (possibly with instruments *colla parte* or in octaves, but never replacing the voices). Viadana applied the first combination (C1–C3–C4–F4) to his capella choir.

Compared to the vocally "full" *capella* choir, the ripieno choirs had fewer persons per part (possibly even solo) and the instrumental/vocal disposition was somewhat freer. The rule that at least one part per choir be vocal was observed, among other things to ensure the continuity of the text, for the high and low choirs sometimes took over sections of the text from the *capella* when it fell silent. In this Vespers this is not so relevant because the ripieno choirs always sing together with the *capella,* but it is still advisable to maintain the rule. Text underlay of a part by no means implies that the part must per se be sung. Purely instrumental parts are sometimes underlaid with text for the practical purpose of enabling the player to "follow" what is going on.

Viadana indicates what sorts of instrumental and vocal combinations are to be employed in his Vespers both in the partbooks and in the preface. The partbooks for Choirs I and II are marked to be for the voices with no indications of instrumentation; those of Choir II are further distinguished by the term "Capella." In his preface, Viadana comments generally on the presence of instruments in these two choirs. For Choirs III and IV, specific indications of instruments and voices are found on the first two pages of each partbook. Following is a list of those indications. The descriptions of the instrumental and vocal combinations for the parts in these choirs are also specific in the preface, and these have been provided below as well (in parentheses) since there are some notable differences between them and the partbook indications.[28] For Choir III, then, the indications and descriptions for the four parts are: Cornetto ò Violino ("sonato da Cornetto, ò Violino"); Voce è Cornetto ò Violino ("cantato da una più buona voce, ò da due, ò da tre di Soprano"); Voce è Violino all'ottava ò Storto ("cantato da più voci e Violini, e Cornetti storti"); Voce è Trombone ("cantato da più voci, con Tromboni, e Violoni, e Organo all'Ottava alta"). For Choir IV: Voce è storto, o Violino all'ottava ("cantato da più voci, con Violini all'ottava, e Cornetti storti"); Voce è Trombone ("cantato da più voci, con Tromboni"); Voce è Trombone ("da buone voci, o da Tromboni, e Violini"); Voce è Trombone ò Violone doppio ("cantato da profondi Bassi, con Tromboni, e Violoni doppi, e Fagotti, con Organo all'Ottava bassa").

More needs to be said about the preface, both in itself and as it relates to the partbooks, since it is often misunderstood and therefore incorrectly interpreted. For a correct reading the following remarks may be of help. We must not view the discrepancies between preface and partbooks as being contradictory, but rather as indications of *possible* instrumentation, depending on the forces available. Furthermore, a literal observation of what Viadana writes is often necessary, as for example with the word order in the case of the top voice of Choir IV: "Violini all'ottava, e Cornetti storti"—the violins are an octave higher, but not the cornetts.[29] The organ basses of Choirs III and IV lie an octave apart. One plays in the high register (i.e., relatively higher) and the other in the low register (i.e., relatively lower).[30] Viadana's use of the word "violone/violoni" has on various occasions been mistranscribed as "violine/violini" and accordingly mistranslated as "violins," when in fact Viadana clearly intends the distinction. The only dubious point could be the word "violini" on the baritone part of Choir IV. It is also true of the other voices that "violino" need not necessarily mean a violin, but rather any member of the violin family, especially viola, and even the obscure "tenor violin." This last instrument may be what is intended in the baritone part of Choir IV.

As regards the cornetts: I have not translated "cornetti storti" as "curved cornetts" because there is a separate term, "cornetto curvo," which would normally apply to a treble cornett (which is perhaps meant for the first canto of Choir III, where the word "storto" does not appear), whereas the term "storto" almost certainly implies a tenor cornett. What in my opinion should not be taken literally is Viadana's use of the plural form of these various instruments. This is possibly an Italian usage which does not necessarily imply more than one instrument. In any case, I believe that the use of single instruments is preferable, and note that the plural forms in the preface are all replaced by the singular in the partbooks!

I also believe that the word "è" in the preface cannot be literally intended, for in many cases that would mean in addition to the voice a doubling of wind and stringed instruments, which is inadvisable. It is best to read "è" as "ò" wherever there is more than one instrument to a part. Here again the partbook version is noteworthy: either the second instrument is omitted or the "è" is in fact omitted, so that there is never any question of wind and string scoring of a part.

Finally, if it is not possible for the *choro favorito* to stand by the organ, the continuo part may be played on a harpsichord, if necessary with a violone, bassoon, or dulcian in the ripieno passages.

The Basso generale

Although the idea of the *basso generale* or *continuo* took form via contributions from various composers and stylistic outlooks, the continuo devised by Viadana in his famous *Cento concerti ecclesiastici* had so much influence on this process, particularly in church music, that he created an international sensation with it, was labelled even by his contemporaries as its "inventor," and finally (as noted previously) went down in history as such. We can see what an arduous process this was from the *basso generale* of this Vespers, which still leans heavily on the already familiar *basso seguente* practice of the polyphonic works from which it evolved (see the organ basses for Choirs III and IV), and from which it increasingly frees itself as it develops into an independent continuo. The figured-bass numbering that had already appeared in monody is missing here. Viadana notates only flat or sharp to indicate a minor or major chord respectively, and even that is done rather haphazardly.

In the continuo partbook one finds copious comments at the beginning of the verse sections giving the instrumentation;[31] this was intended not only for the organist but also for the director, both of whom performed from this *basso generale* part. For a stylistically accurate performance one finds guidance in the preface of the *Cento concerti,* in which Viadana also provides instructions for the organist.[32]

For only one passage does Viadana give advice on organ registration in Psalm 116, measures 1–65: "Principale ottava è quintadecima" (8', 4', and 2', respectively). In his Marian Vespers Monteverdi builds up the registration from "Principale" with solo or a few voices, to "Principale, Ottava è Quintadena" with more voices, up to "Organo pleno" (plenum) for tutti. The use of reeds and 16' stops in the plenum is inadvisable in this style. Viadana says in the *Cento concerti* that in tutti passages the organist may play "with hands and feet."

Pieno (abbreviated as P. in the source) does not always mean "tutti." From measure 33 of Psalm 111 and measure 26 of Psalm 121, for example, by no means all voices are singing. Conversely, *Vuoto* (V.) does not always mean that only a few voices are singing; see, for example, measures 50–54 of Psalm 121. The organist must go through the entire score himself and decide the registration according to his own judgment.

A problem that arises in the source with respect to the *basso generale* is that often it sounds as all other voices rest. When this occurs in the midst of or just before a tutti passage (such as in mvt. II, m. 24, where the *basso generale* has a second semibreve entering beneath a minim rest in all other parts), it seems that in principle the continuo should conform with the voices. However, this sort of discrepancy also occurs in passages for only a few voices or a single choir (such as in mvt. III, m. 98, where the *basso generale* enters as the voices of Choir I observe a minim pause), where the sharp articulation of rests between vocal statements is less of an issue. It has therefore been decided that in this edition the notes of the *basso generale* will be presented as they are found in the source, but that the following instances where they might be altered in performance should be cited (unless otherwise noted, all occurring within or before a tutti passage). Mvt. II: m. 24, note 2; m. 38, note 6; m. 56, note 1; m. 72, note 1; m. 75, note 2; m. 89, note 2. Mvt. III: m. 34, note 2; m. 38, note 1; m. 71, note 1; m. 122, note 3. Mvt. IV: m. 33, note 1 (Choirs I and II only); m. 71, note 3. Mvt. VIII: m. 5, note 3. Mvt. IX: m. 15, note 1; m. 67, note 5; m. 73, note 1. Mvt. X: m. 18, note 3; m. 21, note 1. Mvt. XIb: m. 99, note 3; m. 116, note 3.

Parallel fifths between the vocal parts and the continuo occur fairly frequently; these are not so surprising in this style, with its many root position chords. Viadana even sanctions them in rule 9 of his *Cento concerti ecclesiastici.* However, the same rule forbids parallel fifths and octaves between the vocal parts. The parallel octaves within one and the same choir in Psalm 110, Choir I, measure 72 (between the canto and the quinto), although mitigated by the rest, are without doubt a slip of the pen. Apart from a few unfortunate passages (for example, Psalm 126, measure 12, with parallel fifths between quinto and basso), Viadana proves himself to be a skillful contrapuntalist.

Practices of Variable Forces ad Libitum

The Addition of Complementary Choirs

In his preface Viadana explicitly indicates the performance practices then in fashion: ostentatious effects are achieved through doubling the choirs ("radoppi il Secondo, Terzo, e Quarto Choro"). In fact these practices had been known in Italy since the time of Gabrieli: in order to augment sonority and contrast, particularly in tutti passages, extra choral groups spread throughout the building were added. Doublings, octave doublings, or new independent parts were specially written out for this purpose.

In this connection a comment of Praetorius on Giovanni Gabrieli's works is noteworthy. After describing how extra parts for complementary choirs were written on the basis of the existing parts, Praetorius says that he had seen such extra parts for supplementary choirs written out in the original copies of Gabrieli's works, but that these parts no longer appeared in the printed edition of 1615.[33] In the preface to his *Salmi concertati* Giacobbi also describes various performance options, from the simplest two-choir version (five or six "concertato" voices with organ) to what he calls a "fully-fledged concerto":

> In the main churches, where enough singers and players are available, the judicious director may add further choirs, high and low, each one according to the suitability and appropriateness of the building and according to the number of singers and players available. Everything will be achieved with all the more effect if the distances at which the supplementary choirs are placed from the main choirs are effectively chosen.[34]

Giovanni Ghizzolo offers similar alternative forces in his works for double choir. If there is a shortage of singers he suggests a group of only five voices, with Choir II functioning as an instrumental "forte register"; after that he suggests larger-scale combinations.[35] Praetorius cites the Venetian composer Capello, who also advises the doubling of choirs, particularly in the ripieni.[36] That these Italian practices found their way into Germany is proven by the works of Schütz. In his *Musicalische Exequien*, Schütz advises that the parts for Choir II be copied once or twice, and in his *Symphoniae sacrae* (volume III), he printed parts for a four-voice complementary choir, stating that these themselves could be duplicated for a second choir.[37]

Unison and Octave Doubling

Another practice very much in use was unison and octave doubling of the single voices within a particular choir. As with organ registration, the sung voices were reinforced instrumentally at the unison, octave, and double octave, above and below. The scale of possible shades that this technique offered was the "palette" on which was based the renowned coloring of the Venetian style.

Praetorius states emphatically that all parts, including the middle voices, could be doubled at the unison and octave. He begins the discussion of this topic with the title: "Why in fact not only the discant and bass but also the middle voices in the full choir may sing well and without vitiation in unison, and also sometimes in octaves."[38] He does draw a distinction between unison and octave doubling, however, stating that while the former can be used without hesitation, one must "proceed somewhat more sensibly and carefully" [etwas vernünftiger und säuberlicher umbgehen] with the latter. "Octaves may be tolerated in all voices, [as long as] when one voice sings, the other is played" [Octavae in omnibus vocibus tolerari

possunt: quando una vox cantat, altera sonat].[39] One of his examples is a low choir in which an alto sings against three trombones,[40] the voice being doubled an octave higher by a violin. In the *capella* choir it was usual with the alto voice in particular to double instrumentally at the octave, which gives rise to unavoidable parallel fifths with the soprano line, above which the instrument moves. This was an Italian practice which Praetorius "cannot yet condone" [noch zur zeit nicht beypflichten kan].[41] Yet he supports the latest Italian innovation of singing in unisons and parallel octaves, the very practice that Viadana defends in the last two paragraphs of his preface. Praetorius writes:

> I have heard recently from Venice that the most distinguished musicians in Italy assiduously employ unisons and octaves in the ripieni, having learned from their own experience that in such large churches, where the choirs are far away from one another, they are much stronger if they move together with the other choirs in unison or octaves.[42]

With regard specifically to the bass line, Praetorius refers to its support by 8' and 16' registration on the organ and goes on to speak of specific instruments:

> Therefore the full choir also produces a wonderful harmony if one adds to the bass, since a wide array of instruments is here available, a common or bass trombone, a *Chorist*-bassoon or shawm, doubling the bass at the right pitch, and in addition a double bass trombone, double bassoon, or large double shawm, and a double bass, sounding at the same time an octave below, like the sub-bass or major bass of an organ; which is customary and fairly defensible in today's Italian concertos.[43]

Contemporaries of Praetorius unanimously advocated the reinforcement of the bass in all choirs, although Schütz, when he recommended a double bass viol for the *choro favorito* to double the 16' organ stop, cautioned that such low instruments in particular must be used "with sharp ears and good judgment" [mit scharffen Gehör und gutem Verstande] and discretion.[44] In sum, then, for both the *choro favorito* and the *capella*, 8' reinforcement may be taken as the starting point, with 16' reinforcement reserved for the tutti sections.

Placement

There are countless exhortations in both Italian and German sources to set the choirs as far apart from one another as possible for optimal spatial effect. In works for four choirs a crosswise placement is often advised (see figure 1). With regard to the instruments used to play with the voices of the choirs, if one opts in principle for cornetts in Choir III and trombones in Choir IV, then it is appropriate to have strings play with the *capella* choir (to provide further contrast with the wind instruments of the ripieno choirs). Figure 1 shows that if this is done, the instruments of Choirs III and IV are placed behind the singers while those of Choir II are placed in front (since as mentioned in note 39, winds should be kept behind so as not to overwhelm the voices).

Choir I (*choro favorito*)

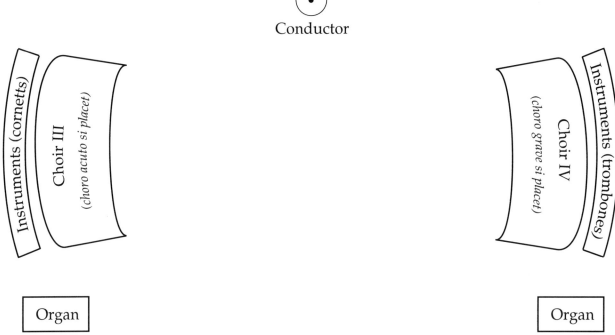

Figure 1. Possible placement of choirs and instruments

Not only are the choirs spread out through the building, but the single voices of the *choro favorito* are as well. This aims at spatial effect and improved differentiation of the voices, particularly if two voices of the same category are singing (for example, a duet for two tenors). This technique, *per cantar lontano,* was tried out by Donati in various churches before he introduced it in his *Sacri concentus* (1612): "The voice which is first to sing stands by the organ, the remaining one, two, or three voices standing apart from one another to one side of the organ, invisible to the congregation, in the manner of separated choirs."[45] (In this regard, note Viadana's advice to have the *Sancta Maria* [second Magnificat, mm. 121–36] sung by an unseen soprano.) Praetorius also advocated a placement in which the singers of the *choro favorito* stand far away from one another (though visible), and Giacobbi too declared himself a supporter of this. The method was much imitated.[46]

Notes

1. This edition presents the text of Viadana's preface in transcription and translation.

2. Viadana's *Officium defunctorum* of 1600 (which has been transcribed and prepared for publication by the editor) is still entirely based on this Renaissance principle: all uneven psalm verses are always plainsong; all even verses are in four parts, *falsobordone* alternating with free counterpoint.

3. For the extent to which this was in fact the case, see Hans Heinrich Eggebrecht, "Arten des Generalbasses im frühen und mittleren 17. Jahrhundert," *Archiv für Musikwissenschaft* 14 (1957): 61–82.

4. Ignazio Donati, *Salmi boscarecci concertati a sei voci, con aggiunta, se piace, di altre sei voci, che servono per concerto, e per ripieno doppio, per cantare a più chori . . .* (Venice, 1623).

5. Much of the information in this section is drawn from Jerome Roche, *North Italian Church Music in the Age of Monteverdi* (Oxford: Clarendon Press, 1984), which deals with this material in its first chapters.

6. Thomas Coryat, *Coryat's Crudities* (London, 1611; reprint, New York: The Macmillan Company, 1905), 1:390.

7. The Roman numeral I equals First Vespers, II equals Second Vespers. Epiphany, Pentecost, and Trinity Sunday have Psalms 109, 110, 111, 112, and 116 in First Vespers, and Psalms 109 to 113 in Second Vespers. If Viadana had provided just one polyphonic setting of Psalm 113, he would have encompassed not only the Second Vespers of the said three feast days but also the "ordinary Sunday Vespers" and the Vespers of Easter Sunday (that of Easter being unique in that it is not preceded by a Vespers on Saturday night because of the long vigil held then), which also have Psalms 109 to 113. Ascension has the same psalms (109, 110, 111, 112, 116) in both Vespers, Circumcision likewise (109, 112, 121, 126, 147). This indicates that Viadana did not have the "ordinary" Sundays of the church year in mind, but the important feasts (as stated on the title page [see plate 1]: "nelle gran Solennità di tutto l'Anno"), and also makes it clear that First Vespers was intended, being traditionally celebrated in extended form on the eve of the feast; for otherwise Viadana would certainly have added that one setting of Psalm 113 to his set.

8. Second Vespers of several male saints' feasts are also attainable within Viadana's psalms. Often it is the last psalm that differentiates First and Second Vespers. The Commune of the Martyrs, for instance, has Psalms 109, 110, 111, 112, and 115 at Second Vespers. Thus with the addition of Psalm 115 to Viadana's collection, the large category of the Martyrs would have become eligible for Second Vespers. Here too the preference seems to be for First Vespers.

9. On Marian feasts both Vespers were often celebrated.

10. Stephen Bonta, "Liturgical Problems in Monteverdi's Marian Vespers," *Journal of the American Musicological Society* 20 (1967): 87–106.

11. That Viadana did not have plainsong antiphons in mind may also be seen from the relatively large number of psalm settings in the tritus (the fifth or sixth) modes; these particular lydian modes are very rare in the antiphon repertoire. Viadana does not conform to lydian modality but to the major-minor tonality that was rapidly gaining ground in his day. Thus the fitful compilation of modally conformant plainsong antiphons is by no means historically or liturgically authentic. Furthermore, it raises another problem. In Viadana's *Officium defunctorum* the plainsong antiphons are printed because these are always the same. Not only do these antiphons seem to deviate melodically to a considerable degree from the version in our plainsong books, but sometimes they are even in an entirely different mode.

12. Adriano Banchieri, *L'Organo suonarino . . . per alternar coristi à gli canti fermi in tutte le feste, & sollennita dell'anno* (Venice, 1605). This work has been reprinted at least six times. Various composers wrote similar works for Mass and/or Vespers, an indication of how intensively the practice of substituting instrumental pieces for antiphons was followed in Italy.

13. Banchieri, *L'Organo suonarino,* 58.

14. Giovanni Gabrieli's ensemble works were also written for the church. The number of published collections exclusively containing instrumental works of this sort (sonatas, canzonas, ricercares) grew enormously after 1600 and was certainly associated with these liturgical practices; the number of Vespers publications also shot up during this time.

15. The Vespers described by Coryat lasted not less than three hours; see note 6.

16. See Bonta, "Liturgical Problems," 101.

17. The hymn may be for one or more soloists and/or choirs, with instrumental accompaniment.

18. *Completorium romanum . . .* (Venice, 1606) is also being prepared for publication in a transcription by the author.

19. After Psalm 4: "Qui si fa un Concerto." After the eleventh verse of Psalm 90: "Qui se la Musica fosse alterata l'organista sonata un poco solo facendo la cadenza in Tuono."

20. Girolamo Giacobbi, *Prima parte de salmi concertati a due e più chori . . .* (Venice, 1609).

21. See Jerome Roche, "What Schütz learnt from Grandi in 1629," *Musical Times* 113 (1972): 1074–75.

22. Point 11 of the preface reads: "In these concertos, falsettos will have a better effect than natural sopranos; because boys, for the most part, sing carelessly, and with little grace, likewise because we have reckoned on distance to give greater charm; there is, however, no doubt that no money can pay a good natural soprano; but there are few of them." See Oliver Strunk, *Source Readings in Music History*, vol. 3, *The Baroque Era* (London: Faber and Faber, 1981), 62.

23. See Ignazio Donati, *Ecclesiae metropolitanae urbini musicae prefecti sacri concentuus unis, binis, ternis, quaternis, & quinis vocibus, una cum parte organica . . .* (Venice, 1612).

24. Strunk, *Source Readings*, 62 n. 2. Strunk offers as an example Viadana's motet "O sacrum convivium," *à voci pari*, with the clefs C3–C4–C4–F4. Viadana's Office for the Dead, written for *Quattuor paribus vocibus*, as stated in the Latin title, has the clefs C2,3–C3,4–F3,4.

25. Michael Praetorius, *Syntagma musicum*, volume III (Wolfenbüttel, 1619; facsimile edition, Documenta musicologica, Kassel: Bärenreiter, 1958).

26. In Germany there was a preference in polychoral works for a homogeneous timbre "per choros," that is, groups of instruments drawn from the same family for a specific choir, hence Praetorius's references to *Flöten Chor, Violen Chor, Posaunen Chor*, etc. The Italians were more inclined to score per part, but in practice the differences are not so great. In Italy the concept of particular timbre groups had been known since the two Gabrielis; and Praetorius, who often considered a mixture of timbres within one group possible or necessary, liked to report the latest Italian developments in his writings.

27. "Besides cornetts only or violins only the following is also possible: one violin and two cornetts; two violins and one cornett; one violin, one cornett, and one flute or recorder." Praetorius, *Syntagma musicum* III, 155. (N.B. It is inadvisable to double a part with cornett and violin.)

28. The explanation of these discrepancies lies in performance practice. The size of a *Kapelle* was subject to sharp alterations according to economic, political, and social circumstances. The musicians in the service of a church were not a true reflection of this in that forces were often hired on a permanent or temporary basis from the city, the court, or a fraternity.

29. The translation "with violins and (curved) cornetts an octave higher" is incorrect. In the partbook "o Violino all'ottava" is preceded by a comma. See also the partbook for the alto of Choir III.

30. Translations such as "an octave higher than usual," and "an octave lower than normal" offer superfluous additions that could be misleading; both organs play in the "usual" or "normal" range.

31. Such as: "A Cinque"; "Basso solo"; "A3, Due Tenori e Basso"; "A4, Choro della Capella"; "A3, Canto Alto è Tenor"; etc. (see plate 3). With the composition now presented in score these comments became superfluous and were in almost all cases omitted.

32. The entire preface is translated in Strunk, *Source Readings*, 59–63. From these instructions certain principles employed in the transcription become clear. For example, Viadana states in point 5 that "When a concerto begins after the manner of a fugue, the organist begins also with a single note [*un tasto solo*], and, on the entry of the several parts, it is at his discretion to accompany them as he pleases." This style of playing is characteristically intended in a passage such as that in the second Magnificat, measures 41–42, hence the editorial addition of "tasto solo." Two further documents are of great importance in this connection, as they were written under the direct influence of Viadana. The first, by Agostino Agazzari, a fiery supporter of the continuo method invented by his friend Viadana, is *Del sonare sopra il basso . . .* (Siena, 1607), also translated in *Source Readings*, 64–71. The second, by Galeazzo Sabbatini, is *La regola facile et breve per suonare sopra il basso continuo . . .* (Venice, 1628). Sabbatini worked in Pesaro, and F. X. Haberl, in "Lodovico Grossi da Viadana: eine bio-bibliographische Studie," *Kirchenmusikalisches Jahrbuch* 4 (1889): 62, says on this subject: "Fano, where Viadana was director in 1612, is not far from Pesaro, and it may be assumed that Sabbatini had lessons in continuo playing from Viadana himself." A comment in Sabbatini's preface also suggests this. Among more recent literature the following writings are important. F. T. Arnold, *The Art of Accompaniment from a Thorough-bass* (London: Dover, 1931; revised 1965). (N.B. In this book Arnold discusses the possibility that Viadana may have used figures. The article "Did Viadana use Figures?" appeared independently in *Musical Times* 63 [1922]: 505–8, followed by a discussion in "Letters to the Editor," 648–49. Nothing of this is seen in this Vespers.) Tharald Borgir, "The Performance of the Basso Continuo in Seventeenth-Century Italian Music" (Ph.D. diss., University of California, Berkeley, 1971). Helmut Haack, *Die Anfänge des Generalbass-Satzes: die 'Cento concerti ecclesiastici' (1602) von Lodovico Viadana* (Tutzing: Hans Schneider, 1974). See also Imogene Horsley, "Full and Short Scores in the Accompaniment of Italian Church Music in the Early Baroque," *JAMS* 30 (1977): 466–99.

33. "And such have I seen many times and in various forms in several of Giovanni Gabrieli's transcribed Concertos; which however are not included among those which have appeared in print in recent years." Praetorius, *Syntagma musicum* III, 114.

34. Giacobbi, *Prima parte di salmi concertati*. Giacobbi's preface is cited by Praetorius in *Syntagma musicum* III, 106, 107, 111, 119, and 191.

35. Giovanni Ghizzolo, *Messa, salmi lettanie falsibordoni concertati a 5 e 9 voci servandosi del secondo choro à beneplacito, con il basso per organo . . .* (Venice, 1619).

36. See Praetorius, *Syntagma musicum* III, 241–42.

37. See Heinrich Schütz, *Musicalische Exequien, IIIe Ordinantz, art. 3* (Dresden, 1636) and *Symphoniae sacrae*, volume III (Dresden, 1650). To sum up, Praetorius states that in general when "a large company of musicians" is available, one must "have the ripieni copied twice or three times and distributed in choirs placed at varying distances from one another." *Syntagma musicum* III, 111.

38. "Warumb nemblich nicht allein der Discant und Bass, sondern auch die MittelStimmen, in pleno Choro zugleich mit einander in Unisonum, und auch zuweiln in Octaven, gar wol und ohne Beschuldigung der Vitiositet gesetzt werden können." Praetorius, *Syntagma musicum* III, 91.

39. Praetorius, *Syntagma musicum* III, 95. For the audibility of the sung text, doubling is advisable in *colla parte* so that the wind instruments never take precedence over the singers. For the same reason, wind instruments should not be placed before the singers but behind them.

40. This applies to Choir IV of Viadana's Vespers, which correspond in structure to Giacobbi's Psalms. Giacobbi advises that in this low choir the highest part (alto) be assigned to voice, the others to "trombones, violins, or something of that sort." See *Prima parte di salmi concertati*.

41. Praetorius, *Syntagma musicum* III, 95.

42. "Es ist mir auch newlich aus Venedig zugeschrieben worden, dass die vornembsten Musici in Italia in den Ripieni . . . mit allem fleiss die Unisonos und Octaven gebrauchen, aus eigener Expirientz und Erfahrung, dass solche Arten in so grossen Kirchen, da die Chor weit von einander seyn, viel bessere Krafft geben, wenn sie mit den andern Choren zugleich in Unisonos oder Octaven fortgehen." Praetorius, *Syntagma musicum* III, 97–98.

43. "Daher es auch in pleno Choro gar eine prächtige Harmoniam von sich gibt, wenn man zu einem Basse, do die menge der Instrumentisten vorhanden, eine gemeine oder Quart-Posaun, ein ChoristFagott, oder PommerBombard, welche den Bass im rechten Thon, Und darneben ein OctavPosaun, doppel Fagott, oder gross doppel Bombard, und gross Bassgeyg,

welche gleich, wie ein Orgeln die SubBässe oder Untersätze, eine Octav drunter Intonirn, anordnet; Welches dann in den jetzigen Italiänischen Concerten gar gebräuchlich, und gnugsam zu verantworten ist." Praetorius, *Syntagma musicum* III, 96.

44. Schütz, *Musicalische Exequien*.

45. Donati, *Ecclesiae metropolitanae urbini musicae prefecti sacri concentuus*.

46. See Praetorius, *Syntagma musicum* III, 172, 176, and 177; and Giacobbi, *Prima parte di salmi concertati*.

Texts and Translations

The English translations of the biblical texts are based on the King James Version of the Bible. The translation of the text of the "Sinfonia a doi tenori" is by the editor.

I. Deus in adjutorium

Deus in adjutorium meum intende.
Domine ad adjuvandum me festina.
Gloria Patri et Filio et Spiritui Sancto.
Sicut erat in principio et nunc et semper, et in saecula saeculorum. Amen. Alleluia.
Laus tibi Domine Rex aeternae gloriae.

O God, turn to me in my adversity.
Make haste to help me, O Lord.
Glory be to the Father and to the Son and to the Holy Ghost.
As it was in the beginning and is now and ever shall be, world without end. Amen. Alleluia.
Praise to thee, O Lord, King of eternal glory.

II. Dixit Dominus (Psalm 109)

Dixit Dominus Domino meo: Sede a dextris meis.
Donec ponam inimicos tuos; scabellum pedum tuorum.
Virgam virtutis tuae emittet Dominus ex Sion; dominare in medio inimicorum tuorum.
Tecum principium in die virtutis tuae in splendoribus sanctorum; ex utero ante luciferum genui te.

Juravit Dominus et non poenitebit eum: Tu es sacerdos in aeternum secundum ordinem Melchisedech.
Dominus a dextris tuis; confregit in die irae suae reges.

Judicabit in nationibus implebit ruinas; conquassabit capita in terra multorum.

De torrente in via bibet; propterea exaltabit caput.

Gloria Patri et Filio; et Spiritui Sancto.
Sicut erat in principio et nunc et semper; et in saecula saeculorum. Amen.

The Lord said unto my Lord, Sit thou at my right hand, until I make thine enemies thy footstool.
The Lord shall send the rod of thy strength out of Zion: rule thou in the midst of thine enemies.
Thy people shall be willing in the day of thy power, in the beauties of holiness from the womb of the morning: thou hast the dew of thy youth.
The Lord hath sworn, and will not repent, Thou art a priest for ever after the order of Melchizedek.
The Lord at thy right hand shall strike through kings in the day of his wrath.
He shall judge among the heathen, he shall fill the places with the dead bodies; he shall wound the heads over many countries.
He shall drink of the brook in the way: therefore shall he left up the head.
Glory be to the Father and to the Son and to the Holy Ghost.
As it was in the beginning and is now and ever shall be, world without end. Amen.

III. Confitebor tibi (Psalm 110)

Confitebor tibi Domine in toto corde meo; in consilio justorum et congregatione.
Magna opera Domini; exquisita in omnes voluntates ejus.
Confessio et magnificentia opus ejus; et justitia ejus manet in saeculum saeculi.
Memoriam fecit mirabilium suorum, misericors et miserator Dominus; escam dedit timentibus se.

I will praise the Lord with my whole heart, in the assembly of the upright, and in the congregation.
The works of the Lord are great, sought out of all them that have pleasure therein.
His work is honorable and glorious: and his righteousness endureth for ever.
He hath made his wonderful works to be remembered: the Lord is gracious and full of compassion. He hath given meat unto them that fear him:

Memor erit in saeculum testamenti sui; virtutem operum suorum annuntiabit populo suo.

Ut det illis haereditatem gentium; opera manuum ejus veritas et judicium.

Fidelia omnia mandata ejus, confirmata in saeculum saeculi; facta in veritate et aequitate.

Redemptionem misit populo suo; mandavit in aeternum testamentum suum.

Sanctum et terribile nomen ejus; initium sapientiae timor Domini.

Intellectus bonus omnibus facientibus eum; laudatio ejus manet in saeculum saeculi.

Gloria Patri et Filio; et Spiritui Sancto.

Sicut erat in principio et nunc et semper; et in saecula saeculorum. Amen.

he will ever be mindful of his covenant. He hath shewed his people the power of his works,

that he may give them the heritage of the heathen. The works of his hands are verity and judgment;

all his commandments are sure. They stand fast for ever and ever, and are done in truth and uprightness.

He sent redemption unto his people: he hath commanded his covenant for ever:

holy and reverend is his name. The fear of the Lord is the beginning of wisdom:

a good understanding have all they that do his commandments: his praise endureth for ever.

Glory be to the Father and to the Son and to the Holy Ghost.

As it was in the beginning and is now and ever shall be, world without end. Amen.

IV. Beatus vir (Psalm 111)

Beatus vir qui timet Dominum; in mandatis ejus volet nimis.

Potens in terra erit semen ejus; generatio rectorum benedicetur.

Gloria et divitiae in domo ejus; et justitia ejus manet in saeculum saeculi.

Exortum est in tenebris lumen rectis; misericors et miserator et justus.

Jucundus homo qui miseretur et commodat, disponet sermones suos in judicio; quia in aeternum non commovebitur.

In memoria aeterna erit justus; ab auditione mala non timebit.

Paratum cor ejus sperare in Domino, confirmatum est cor ejus; non commovebitur donec despiciat inimicos suos.

Dispersit dedit pauperibus, justitia ejus manet in saeculum saeculi; cornu ejus exaltabitur in gloria.

Peccator videbit et irascetur, dentibus suis fremet et tabescet; desiderium peccatorum peribit.

Gloria Patri et Filio; et Spiritui Sancto.

Sicut erat in principio et nunc et semper; et in saecula saeculorum. Amen.

Blessed is the man that feareth the Lord, that delighteth greatly in his commandments.

His seed shall be mighty upon earth: the generation of the upright shall be blessed.

Wealth and riches shall be in his house: and his righteousness endureth for ever.

Unto the upright there ariseth light in the darkness: he is gracious, and full of compassion, and righteous.

A good man sheweth favour, and lendeth: he will guide his affairs with discretion. Surely he shall not be moved for ever:

the righteous shall be in everlasting remembrance. He shall not be afraid of evil tidings:

his heart is fixed, trusting in the Lord. His heart is established, he shall not be afraid, until he see his desire upon his enemies.

He hath dispersed, he hath given to the poor; his righteousness endureth for ever; his horn shall be exalted with honor.

The wicked shall see it, and be grieved; he shall gnash with his teeth, and melt away: the desire of the wicked shall perish.

Glory be to the Father and to the Son and to the Holy Ghost.

As it was in the beginning and is now and ever shall be, world without end. Amen.

V. Laudate pueri (Psalm 112)

Laudate pueri Dominum; laudate nomen Domini.

Sit nomen Domini benedictum; ex hoc nunc et usque in saeculum.

A solis ortu usque ad occasum; laudabile nomen Domini.

Excelsus super omnes gentes Dominus; et super coelos gloria ejus.

Quis sicut Dominus Deus noster qui in altis habitat; et humilia respicit in coelo et in terra?

Praise, O ye servants of the Lord, praise the name of the Lord.

Blessed be the name of the Lord from this time forth and for evermore.

From the rising of the sun unto the going down of the same the Lord's name is to be praised.

The Lord is high above all nations, and his glory above the heavens.

Who is like unto the Lord our God, who dwelleth on high, who humbleth himself to behold the things that are in heaven, and in the earth?

Suscitans a terra inopem; et de stercore erigens pauperem.

Ut collocet eum cum principibus; cum principibus populi sui.

Qui habitare facit sterilem in domo; matrem filiorum laetantem.

Gloria Patri et Filio; et Spiritui Sancto.

Sicut erat in principio et nunc et semper; et in saecula saeculorum. Amen.

He raiseth up the poor out of the dust, and lifteth the needy out of the dunghill;

That he may set him with princes, even with the princes of his people.

He maketh the barren woman to keep house, and to be a joyful mother of children.

Glory be to the Father and to the Son and to the Holy Ghost.

As it was in the beginning and is now and ever shall be, world without end. Amen.

VI. Laudate Dominum (Psalm 116)

Laudate Dominum omnes gentes; laudate eum omnes populi.

Quoniam confirmata est super nos misericordia ejus; et veritas Domini manet in aeternum.

Gloria Patri et Filio; et Spiritui Sancto.

Sicut erat in principio et nunc et semper; et in saecula saeculorum. Amen.

O praise the Lord, all ye nations: praise him, all ye people.

For his merciful kindness is great toward us: and the truth of the Lord endureth for ever.

Glory be to the Father and to the Son and to the Holy Ghost.

As it was in the beginning and is now and ever shall be, world without end. Amen.

VII. Laetatus sum (Psalm 121)

Laetatus sum in his quae dicta sunt mihi: In domum Domini ibimus.

Stantes erant pedes nostri; in atriis tuis Jerusalem.

Jerusalem quae aedificatur ut civitas; cujus participatio ejus in idipsum.

Illuc enim ascenderunt tribus tribus Domini; testimonium Israel ad confitendum nomini Domini.

Quia illic sederunt sedes in judicio; sedes super domum David.

Rogate quae ad pacem sunt Jerusalem; et abundantia diligentibus te.

Fiat pax in virtute tua; et abundantia in turribus tuis.

Propter fratres meos et proximos meos; loquebar pacem de te.

Propter domum Domini Dei nostri; quaesivi bona tibi.

Gloria Patri et Filio; et Spiritui Sancto.

Sicut erat in principio et nunc et semper; et in saecula saeculorum. Amen.

I was glad when they said unto me, Let us go into the house of the Lord.

Our feet shall stand within thy gates, O Jerusalem.

Jerusalem is builded as a city that is compact together:

whither the tribes go up, the tribes of the Lord, unto the testimony of Israel, to give thanks unto the name of the Lord.

For there are set thrones of judgment, the thrones of the house of David.

Pray for the peace of Jerusalem: they shall prosper that love thee.

Peace be within thy walls, and prosperity within thy palaces.

For my brethren and companions' sakes, I will now say, Peace be within thee.

Because of the house of the Lord our God I will seek thy good.

Glory be to the Father and to the Son and to the Holy Ghost.

As it was in the beginning and is now and ever shall be, world without end. Amen.

VIII. Nisi Dominus (Psalm 126)

Nisi Dominus aedificaverit domum; in vanum laboraverunt qui aedificant eam.

Nisi Dominus custodierit civitatem; frustra vigilat qui custodit eam.

Vanum est vobis ante lucem surgere; surgite postquam sederitis qui manducatis panem doloris.

Cum dederit dilectis suis somnum; ecce haereditas Domini filii merces fructus ventris.

Sicut sagittae in manu potentis; ita filii excussorum.

Beatus vir qui implevit desiderium suum ex ipsis; non confundetur cum loquetur inimicis suis in porta.

Except the Lord build the house, they labour in vain that build it:

except the Lord keep the city, the watchman waketh but in vain.

It is vain for you to rise up early, to sit up late, to eat the bread of sorrows:

for so he giveth his beloved sleep. Lo, children are an heritage of the Lord: and the fruit of the womb is his reward.

As arrows are in the hand of a mighty man; so are children of the youth.

Happy is the man that hath his quiver full of them: they shall not be ashamed, but they shall speak with the enemies in the gate.

Gloria Patri et Filio; et Spiritui Sancto.

Sicut erat in principio et nunc et semper; et in saecula saeculorum. Amen.

Glory be to the Father and to the Son and to the Holy Ghost.

As it was in the beginning and is now and ever shall be, world without end. Amen.

IX. Lauda Jerusalem (Psalm 147)

Lauda Jerusalem Dominum; lauda Deum tuum Sion.

Quoniam confortavit seras portarum tuarum; benedixit filiis tuis in te.

Qui posuit fines tuos pacem; et adipe frumenti satiat te.

Qui emittit eloquium suum terrae; velociter currit sermo ejus.

Qui dat nivem sicut lanam; nebulam sicut cinerem spargit.

Mittit crystallum suam sicut buccellas; ante faciem frigoris ejus quis sustinebit?

Emittet verbum suum et liquefaciet ea; flabit spiritus ejus et fluent aquae.

Qui annuntiat verbum suum Jacob; justitias et judicia sua Israel.

Non fecit taliter omni nationi; et judicia sua non manifestavit eis.

Gloria Patri et Filio; et Spiritui Sancto.

Sicut erat in principio et nunc et semper; et in saecula saeculorum. Amen.

Praise the Lord, O Jerusalem; praise thy God, O Zion.

For he hath strengthened the bars of thy gates; he hath blessed thy children within thee.

He maketh peace in thy borders, and filleth thee with the finest of the wheat.

He sendeth forth his commandment upon earth: his word runneth very swiftly.

He giveth snow like wool: he scattereth the hoarfrost like ashes.

He casteth forth his ice like morsels: who can stand before this cold?

He sendeth out his word, and melteth them: he causeth his wind to blow, and the waters flow.

He sheweth his word unto Jacob, his statutes and his judgments unto Israel.

He hath not dealt so with any nation: and as for his judgments, they have not known them.

Glory be to the Father and to the Son and to the Holy Ghost.

As it was in the beginning and is now and ever shall be, world without end. Amen.

X. Magnificat

Magnificat; anima mea Dominum.

Et exsultavit spiritus meus; in Deo salutari meo.

Quia respexit humilitatem ancillae suae; ecce enim ex hoc beatam me dicent omnes generationes.

Quia fecit mihi magna qui potens est; et sanctum nomen ejus.

Et misericordia ejus a progenie in progenies; timentibus eum.

Fecit potentiam in brachio suo; dispersit superbos mente cordis sui.

Deposuit potentes de sede; et exaltavit humiles.

Esurientes implevit bonis; et divites dimisit inanes.

Suscepit Israel puerum suum; recordatus misericordiae suae.

Sicut locutus est ad patres nostros; Abraham et semini ejus in saecula.

Gloria Patri et Filio; et Spiritui Sancto.

Sicut erat in principio et nunc et semper; et in saecula saeculorum. Amen.

My soul doth magnify the Lord.

And my spirit hath rejoiced in God my Saviour.

For he hath regarded the low estate of his handmaiden: for, behold, from henceforth all generations shall call me blessed.

For he that is mighty hath done to me great things; and holy is his name.

And his mercy is on them that fear him from generation to generation.

He hath shewed strength with his arm; he hath scattered the proud in the imagination of their hearts.

He hath put down the mighty from their seats, and exalted them of low degree.

He hath filled the hungry with good things; and the rich he hath sent empty away.

He hath holpen his servant Israel, in remembrance of his mercy;

as he spake to our fathers, to Abraham, and to his seed for ever.

Glory be to the Father and to the Son and to the Holy Ghost.

As it was in the beginning and is now and ever shall be, world without end. Amen.

XIa. Sinfonia a doi tenori

Plaudat nunc organis Maria et inter articulos veloces timpana puerpere concrepent.

Concinant laetantes chori et alternantibus modulis dulcia carmina misceantur.

Now let Mary play instruments and let the tambourines sound under the quick fingers of the Holy Mary.

Let the choruses gladly unite their singing, and may their antiphonal chant blend into sweet songs.

Audite ergo quemadmodum timpanistria nostra cantaverit.

So hear how our tambourine player has sung.

Ait enim.

For she says.

XIb. Magnificat (see mvt. X)

(Added text of the concealed soprano ["Soprano da nascosto"] in mm. 121–36):

Sancta Maria ora pro nobis.

Holy Mary pray for us.

Plate 1. Lodovico Grossi da Viadana, *Salmi a quattro chori* (Venice, 1612), title page of basso (secondo choro) partbook. Courtesy of the Civico Museo Bibliografico Musicale, Bologna.

Plate 2. Lodovico Grossi da Viadana, *Salmi a quattro chori* (Venice, 1612), first page of Magnificat sexti toni, alto (secondo choro) partbook. Courtesy of the Civico Museo Bibliografico Musicale, Bologna.

Plate 3.   Lodovico Grossi da Viadana, *Salmi a quattro chori* (Venice, 1612), page with start of "Beatus vir," basso generale partbook. Courtesy of the Civico Museo Bibliografico Musicale, Bologna.

Salmi
a quattro chori

Modo di concertare
i detti salmi a quattro chori

Il primo Choro à cinque, starà nell'Organo principale, e sarà il choro favorito, e questo sarà cantato, è recitato da cinque buoni Cantori, che sieno sicuri, franchi, è che cantino alla moderna.

In questo Choro non ci anderà Stromento nessuno, se non l'Organo, e un Chitarone, à chi piace. L'Organista stara vigilante per registrare a luogo, a tempo; e quando troverà queste parole VOTO, e PIENO, doverà registrare, voto; e pieno.

Quando nel detto Choro canterà una voce, due, tre, quattro, cinque; L'Organista sonerà semplice, e schietto, non diminuendo, nè facendo passaggi niente. Ne'Ripieni poi, suonerà come gli piacerà, perchè all'hora è il suo tempo.

Il Secondo Choro à Quattro, sarà la Capella, ove consiste tutto il nervo e fondamento della buona Musica. In questo Choro, non ci vogliono manco di sedeci Cantori, e mancando di tal numero, sarà sempre debil Capella; ma quando saranno venti, è trenta e di Voci e di Stromenti, sara buon corpo di Musica, e farà ottima riuscita.

Il Terzo Choro a Quattro, sarà Acuto: il Primo Canto, come sopranissimo, sarà sonato da Cornetto, ò Violino. Il Secondo sarà cantato da una più buona voce, ò da due, ò da tre di Soprano. L'Alto, è un mezzo Soprano, e sarà cantato da più voci e Violini, e Cornetti storti. Il Tenore sarà ancor'esso cantato da più voci, con Tromboni, e Violoni, e Organo all'Ottava alta.

Il Quarto Choro a Quattro, sarà Grave, cioè à voci pari: Il Soprano, e un'Alto bassissimo, e sarà cantato da più voci, con Violini all'ottava, e Cornetti storti. L'Alto, e un Tenore commodissimo, e sarà cantato da più voci, con Tromboni. Il Tenore, è un Baritone, cioè mezzo Basso, questo ancora doverà esser'accompagnato da buone voci, o da Tromboni, e Violini. Il Basso stà sempre Grave, perciò sarà cantato da profondi Bassi, con Tromboni, e Violoni doppi, e Fagotti, con Organo all'Ottava bassa.

Questi Salmi si possono cantare anco a due Chori soli, cioè Primo è Secondo Choro. Chi volesse poi fare una bella mostra come hoggidì il Mondo si compiace di fare à 4. à 5. à 6. à 7. à 8. Chori, radoppi il Secondo, Terzo, e Quarto Choro, e'havera l'intento suo, senza pericolo nissuno di far'errore; perche tutto il negotio stà in cantar bene il detto Primo Choro à Cinque.

Il Maestro di Capella, starà nell'istesso Choro à Cinque, guardando sempre su'l Basso Continuo dell'Organista, per osservare gli andamenti della Musica, e comandar quando à da cantar'un solo, quando due, quando tre, quando quattro, quando cinque. E quando si faranno i Ripieni, volterà la faccia a tutti i Chori, levando ambe le mani, segno che tutti insieme cantino.

Tutti i Chori per se stessi cantano legitimamente, e tutti hanno le loro consonanze, e separati l'un da l'altro, non si può discernere, se cantano all'Ottava, nè all'unisono. E così io mi son compiaciuto di fare, poiche la Musica riesce assai meglio; perciochè chi vuol comporre osservatamente ne'Ripieni, bisogna servirsi di pause, di mezze

How to arrange
the above-mentioned psalms for four choirs

The first choir, with five voices, stands beside the main organ and is the *choro favorito*, consisting of five good singers who must sing and recite with confidence and boldness, in the modern style.

In this choir no instrument plays apart from organ and, if desired, chitarrone. The organist must take care that at the appropriate moment, at the words *V(u)oto* and *Pieno*, he changes register accordingly.

When one or more voices of this choir are singing, the organist must play simply and clearly, without diminutions and *passagi*. In the ripieni, however, he may play as he wishes, for then he has occasion to do so.

The second, four-part choir is the *capella*, which is the core and the foundation of good music. This choir must consist of at least sixteen singers; with a smaller number it will always be a poor *capella*. But if it consists of twenty or thirty voices and instruments, it is a good ensemble and will sound excellent.

The third choir, in four parts, is a high choir. The first part, a high soprano, is played by cornett or violin. The second part is sung by one, two, or three good sopranos. The alto, a mezzo-soprano part, is performed by several voices with violins and cornetts. The tenor is also performed by several voices, with trombones, violones, and organ in the high register.

The fourth choir, in four parts, is a low choir, that is to say, *à voci pari*: the upper voice is a very low alto, sung by several voices, with violins an octave higher, and cornetts. The second part, in a comfortable tenor range, is sung by several voices, with trombones. The third part is a baritone, and here too a number of good voices are necessary, or trombones and violins. The fourth part is low throughout and must be sung by deep basses, with trombones, double bass violins, and bassoons, and organ in the low register.

These psalms may also be sung by only two choirs, namely first choir and second choir. However, if one wishes to present something beautiful such as people nowadays so like to hear, with four, five, six, seven, and eight choirs, then the second, third, and fourth choirs must be doubled. With such forces there is no danger of things going wrong, for all depends on the good singing of the first five-part choir.

The director must stand in front of this five-part choir, always keeping an eye on the basso continuo, paying attention to the progress of the music and giving the entries for the choir. In the ripieni he must turn his face toward all the choirs and raise both hands to indicate that all should sing together.

All choirs must blend well both singly and together. Because they stand apart from one another the listener cannot distinguish whether they are singing in octaves or in unison. I chose to do it in this way because the music sounds much better thus. For if one wishes to follow the rules strictly in the ripieni, one must introduce whole rests and half rests, dotted notes and syncopations; as a

pause di sospiri, di punti, de sincope, il che fa la Musica stiracchiata, rustica, ed ostinata, cantandosi sempre a rompicollo, e con poca gratia.

So nondimeno, che si trovera qualche bell'humore, che faccendo profession d'orecchia delicata, e purgata, haverà qualche scrupulo intorno à questa novità, benche altri habbiano fatto lo stesso prima di me, come poi si vede in istampa nel Iubilate è Laudate à 16. del Pallavicino, che i Soprani, e i Tenori cantano da 25. ò 30. battute in ottava per movimento congiunto. Ma per finirla, hò fatto a mio modo: così facciano gli altri, poiche adesso è un tempo, che chi fa alla peggio, par che faccia meglio. E Dio sia con voi.

result the music becomes distorted, clumsy, and unyielding, and the singing reckless and less attractive.

Nonetheless I know that here are always a few who know better, who, calling upon their fine and perfect hearing, will complain about this innovation, although others before me have already done the same—as one may see in the printed sixteen-part Jubilate and Laudate by Pallavicino, in which the sopranos and tenors move in parallel octaves for twenty-five to thirty bars. But when all is said and done I have done things my own way. And so do others also, for we live in an age when those who do the worst are regarded as the best. God be with you.

Ranges of Voices

Whole notes show standard ranges; unstemmed noteheads show exceptions.

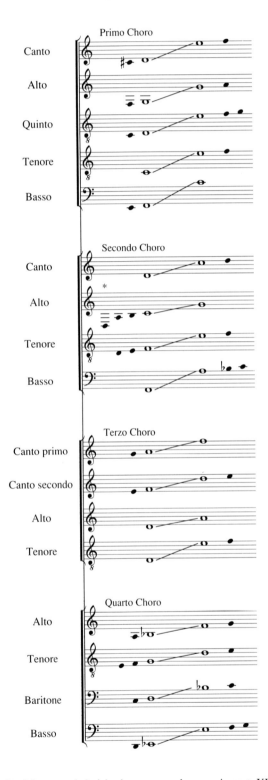

*The low D of the second choir's alto occurs only once, in mvt. XIb, measure 44.

I. Deus in adjutorium

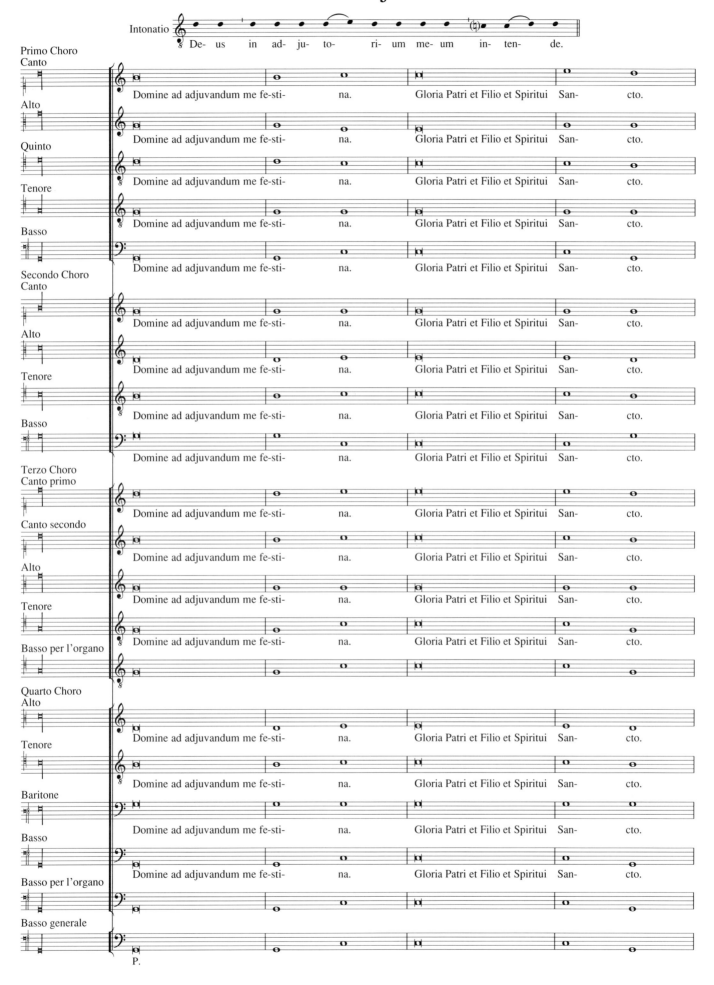

Intonatio
De- us in ad- ju- to- ri- um me- um in- ten- de.

Primo Choro
Canto — Domine ad adjuvandum me fe-sti- na. Gloria Patri et Filio et Spiritui San- cto.
Alto — Domine ad adjuvandum me fe-sti- na. Gloria Patri et Filio et Spiritui San- cto.
Quinto — Domine ad adjuvandum me fe-sti- na. Gloria Patri et Filio et Spiritui San- cto.
Tenore — Domine ad adjuvandum me fe-sti- na. Gloria Patri et Filio et Spiritui San- cto.
Basso — Domine ad adjuvandum me fe-sti- na. Gloria Patri et Filio et Spiritui San- cto.

Secondo Choro
Canto — Domine ad adjuvandum me fe-sti- na. Gloria Patri et Filio et Spiritui San- cto.
Alto — Domine ad adjuvandum me fe-sti- na. Gloria Patri et Filio et Spiritui San- cto.
Tenore — Domine ad adjuvandum me fe-sti- na. Gloria Patri et Filio et Spiritui San- cto.
Basso — Domine ad adjuvandum me fe-sti- na. Gloria Patri et Filio et Spiritui San- cto.

Terzo Choro
Canto primo — Domine ad adjuvandum me fe-sti- na. Gloria Patri et Filio et Spiritui San- cto.
Canto secondo — Domine ad adjuvandum me fe-sti- na. Gloria Patri et Filio et Spiritui San- cto.
Alto — Domine ad adjuvandum me fe-sti- na. Gloria Patri et Filio et Spiritui San- cto.
Tenore — Domine ad adjuvandum me fe-sti- na. Gloria Patri et Filio et Spiritui San- cto.
Basso per l'organo

Quarto Choro
Alto — Domine ad adjuvandum me fe-sti- na. Gloria Patri et Filio et Spiritui San- cto.
Tenore — Domine ad adjuvandum me fe-sti- na. Gloria Patri et Filio et Spiritui San- cto.
Baritone — Domine ad adjuvandum me fe-sti- na. Gloria Patri et Filio et Spiritui San- cto.
Basso — Domine ad adjuvandum me fe-sti- na. Gloria Patri et Filio et Spiritui San- cto.
Basso per l'organo

Basso generale
P.

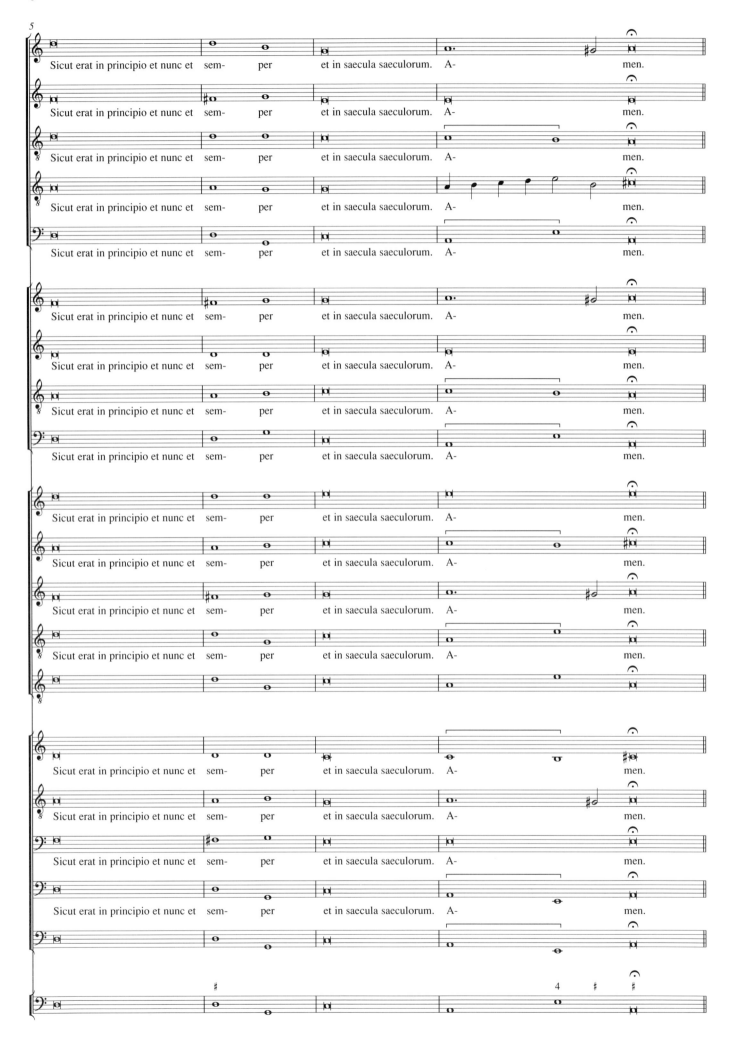

14

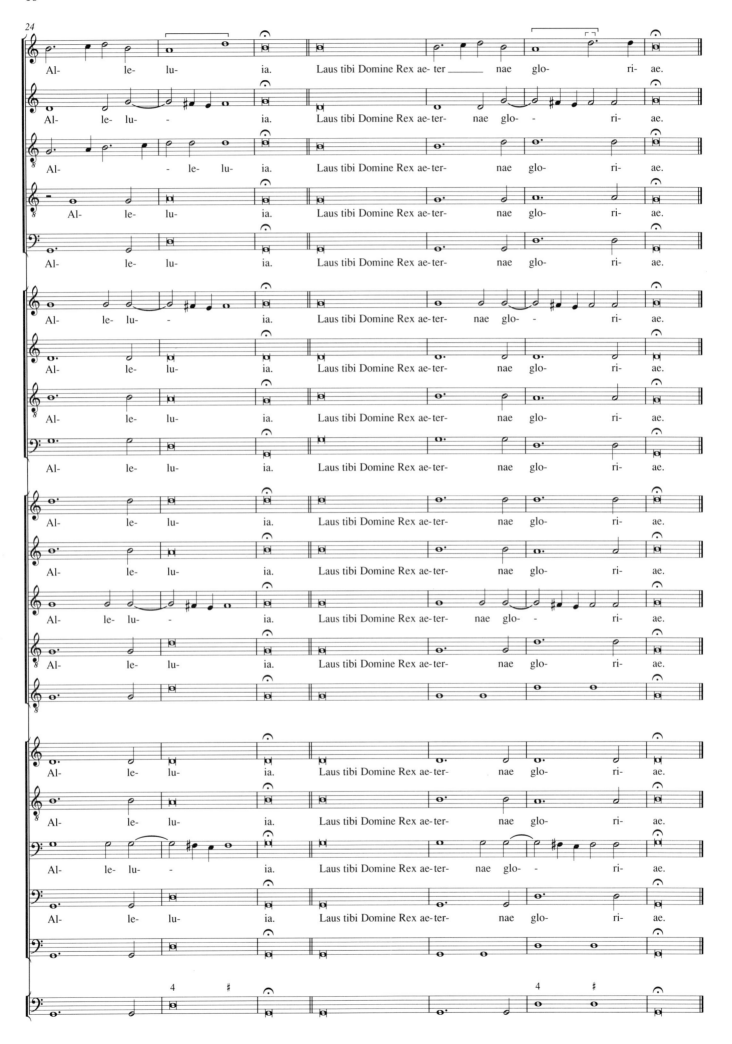

II. Dixit Dominus (Psalm 109)

24

III. Confitebor tibi (Psalm 110)

IV. Beatus vir (Psalm 111)

V. Laudate pueri (Psalm 112)

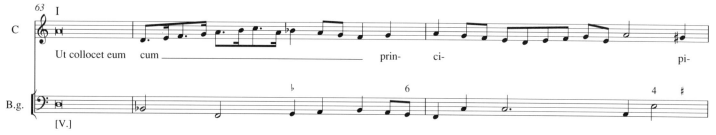

Glo- ri- a Pa- tri et Fi- li- o; et Spi- ri- tu- i San- - cto.

V.

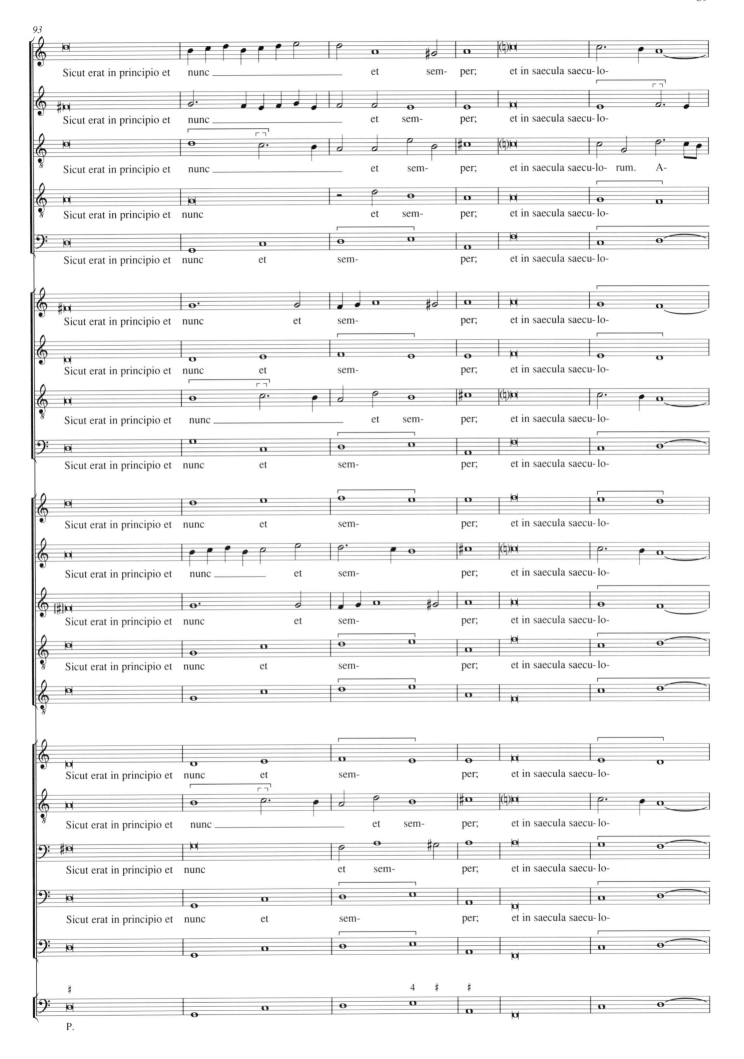

VI. Laudate Dominum (Psalm 116)

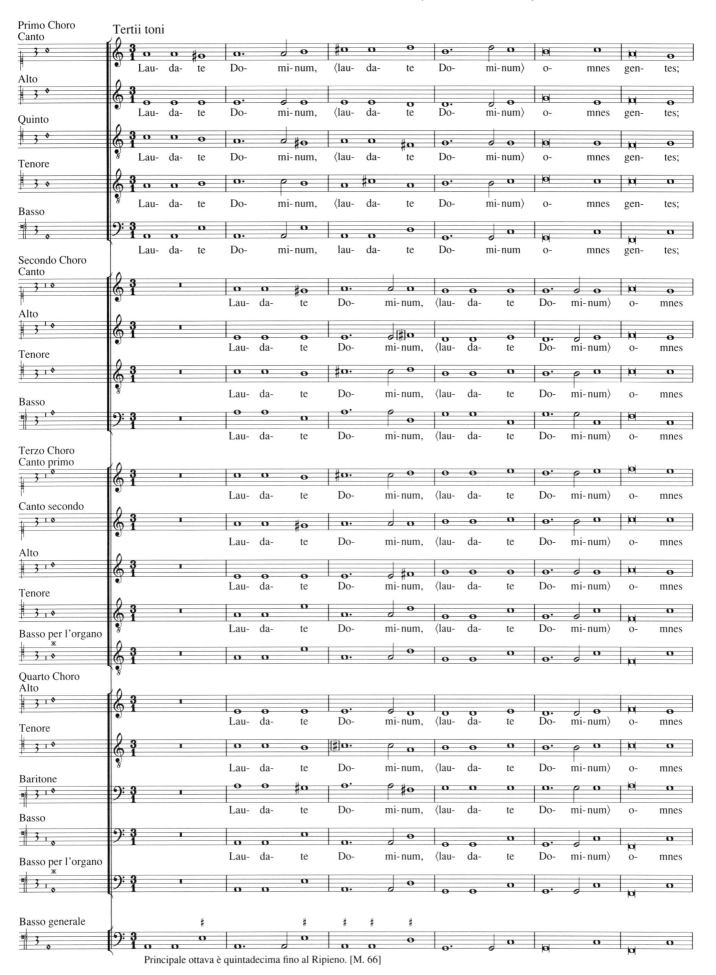

Principale ottava è quintadecima fino al Ripieno. [M. 66]

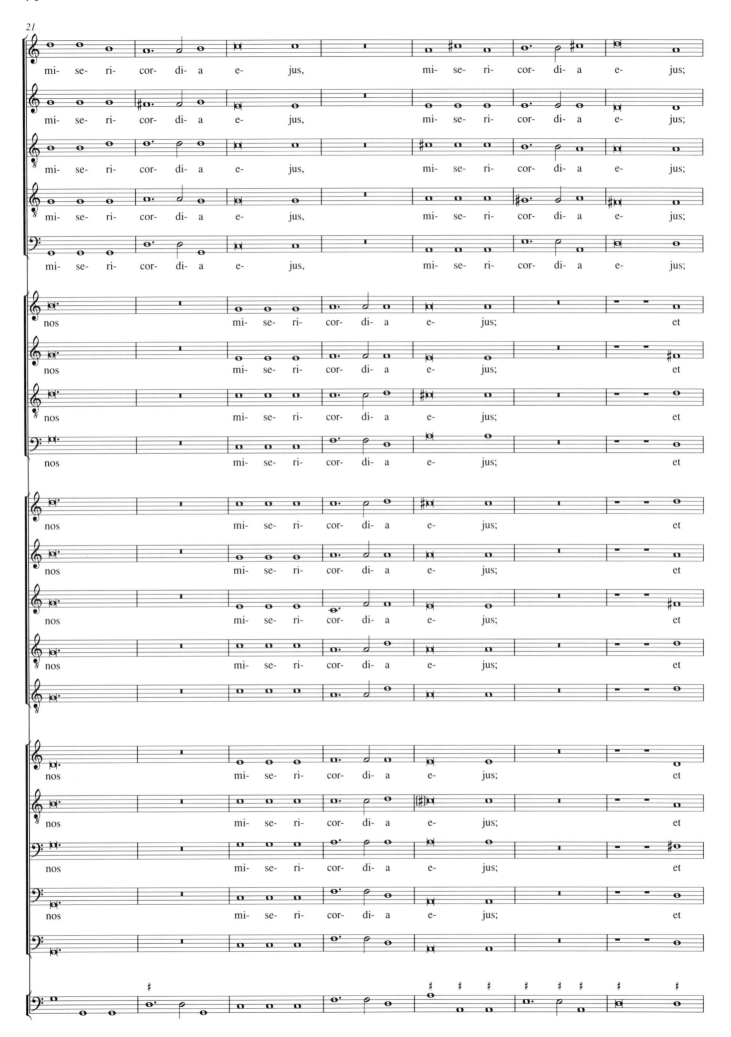

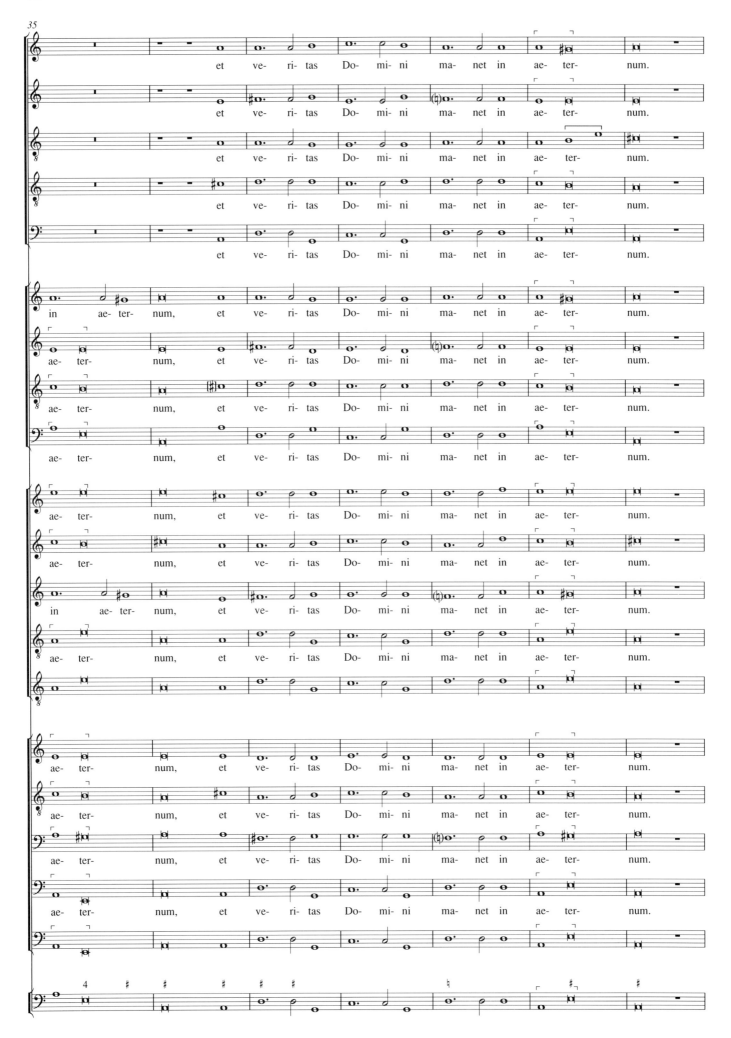

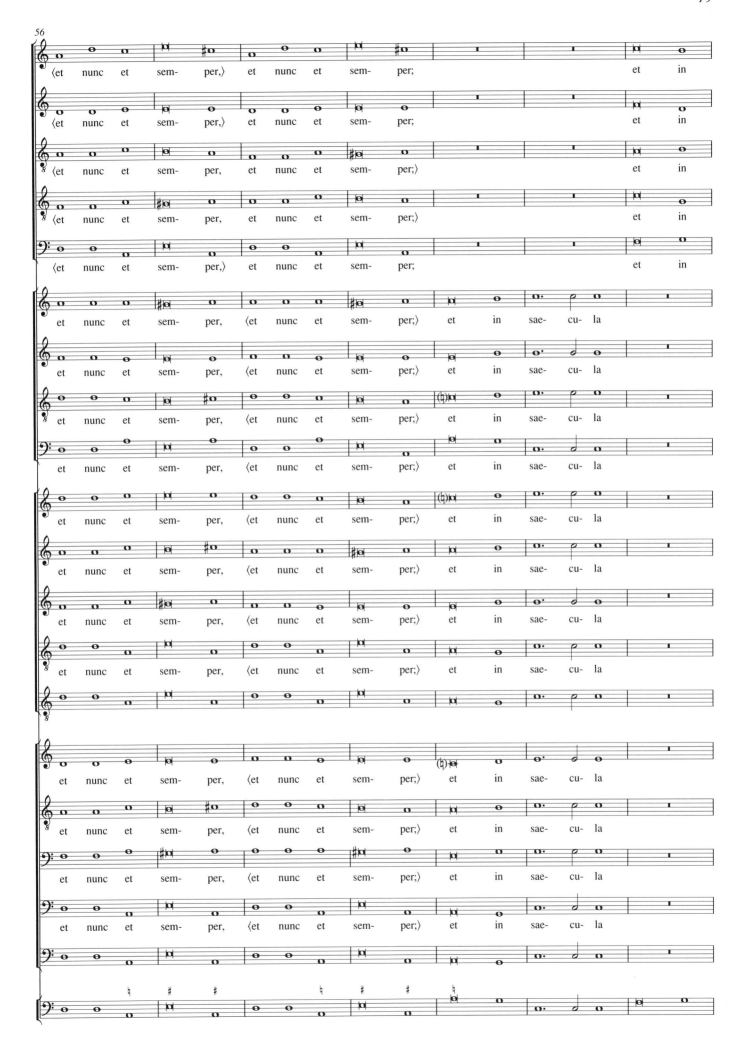

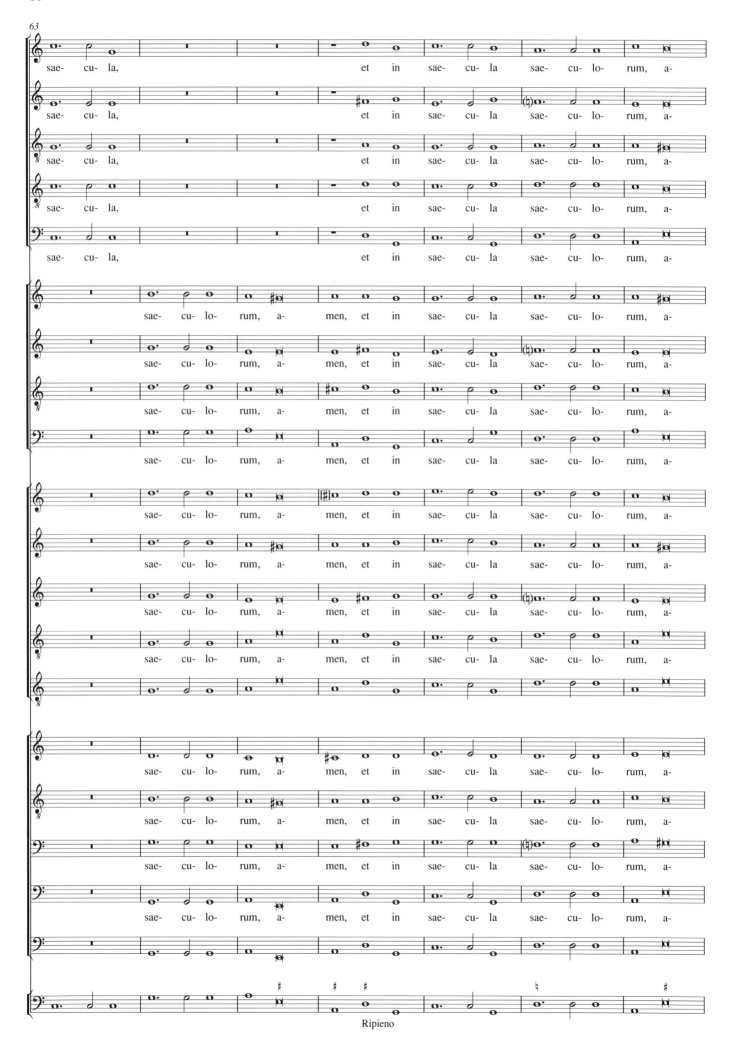

Ripieno

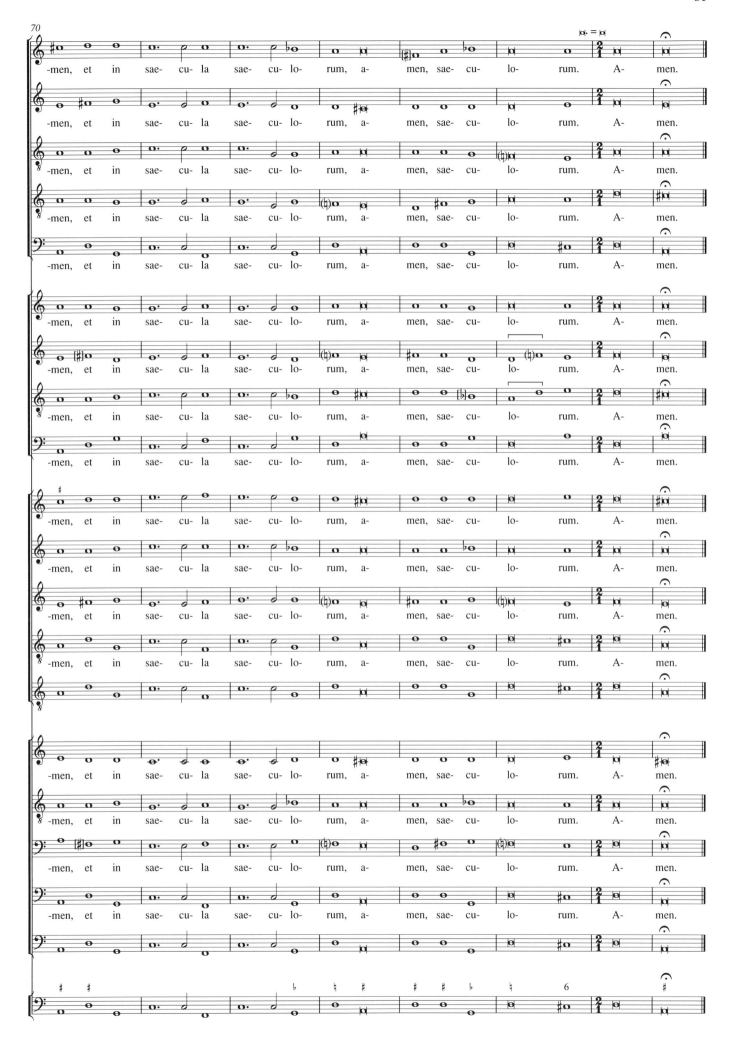

VII. Laetatus sum (Psalm 121)

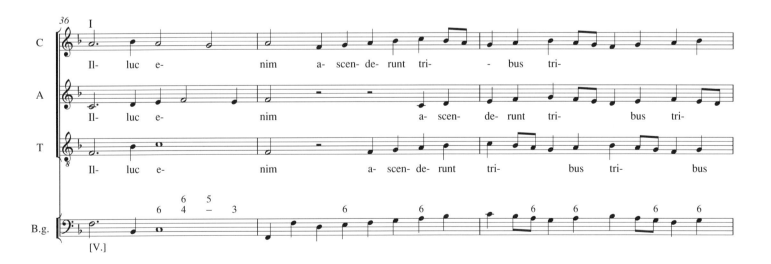

55

60
quae ad pa-cem sunt, ⟨quae ad pa-cem sunt,⟩ quae ad pa-cem sunt, ⟨quae ad pa- cem sunt⟩ Je- ru- sa- lem;
quae ad pa-cem, quae ad pa-cem sunt, quae ad pa-cem, quae ad pa-cem sunt Je- ru- sa-lem;
Ro- ga- te, ro- ga- te quae ad pa-cem sunt Je- ru- sa-lem;
quae ad pa-cem, quae ad pa-cem sunt, quae ad pa-cem sunt Je- ru- - sa- lem;
quae ad pa-cem sunt, quae ad pa-cem sunt Je- ru- - sa- lem;
V.

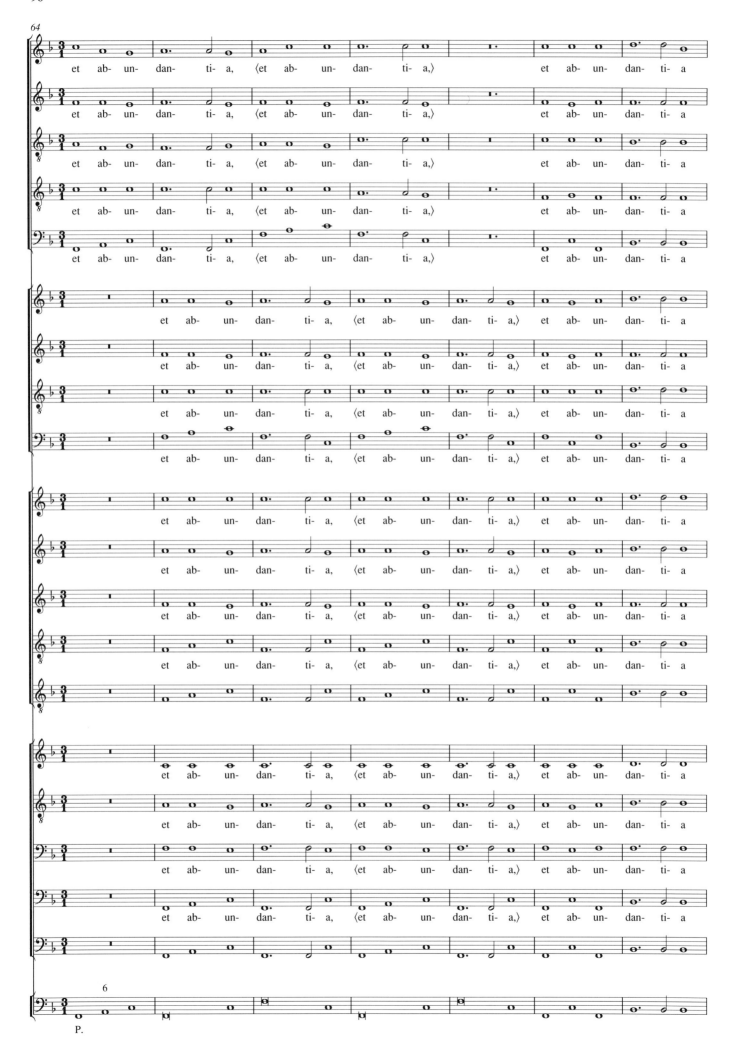

81

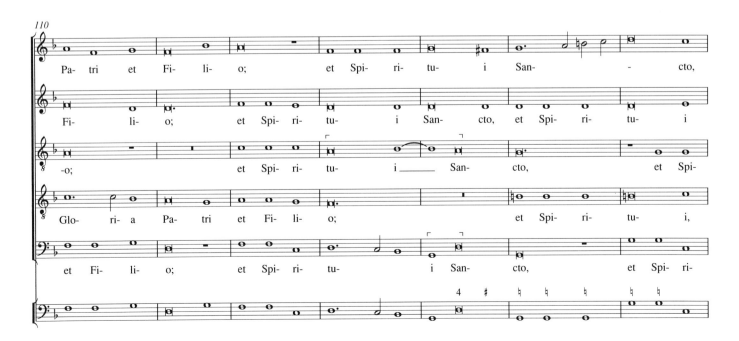

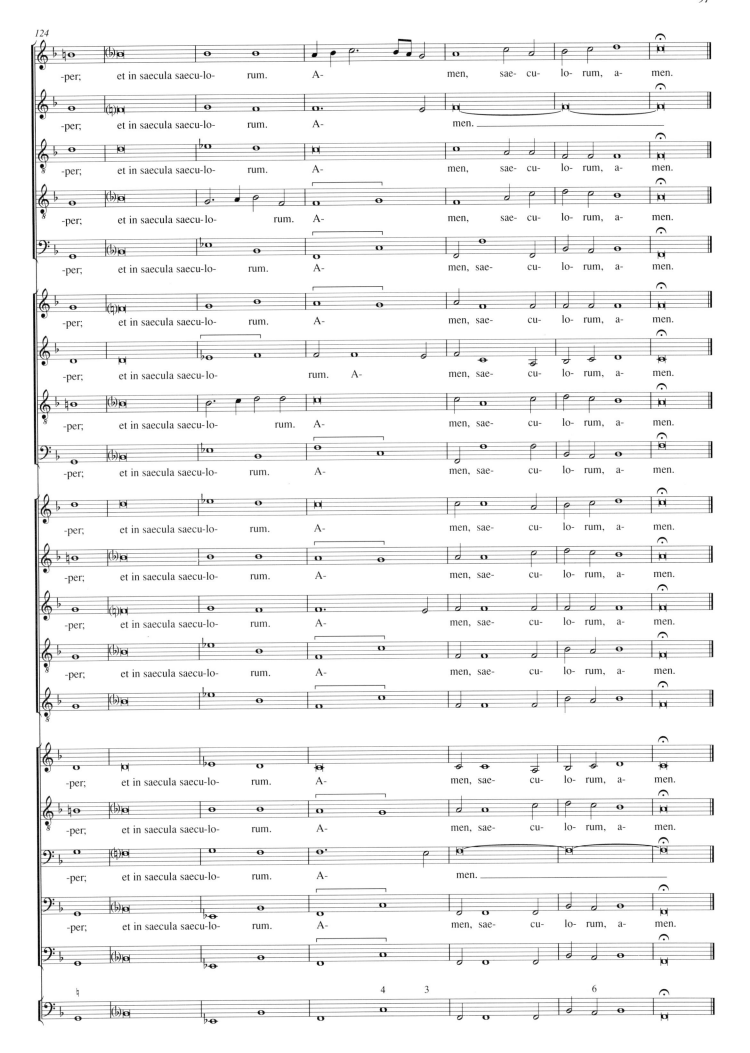

VIII. Nisi Dominus (Psalm 126)

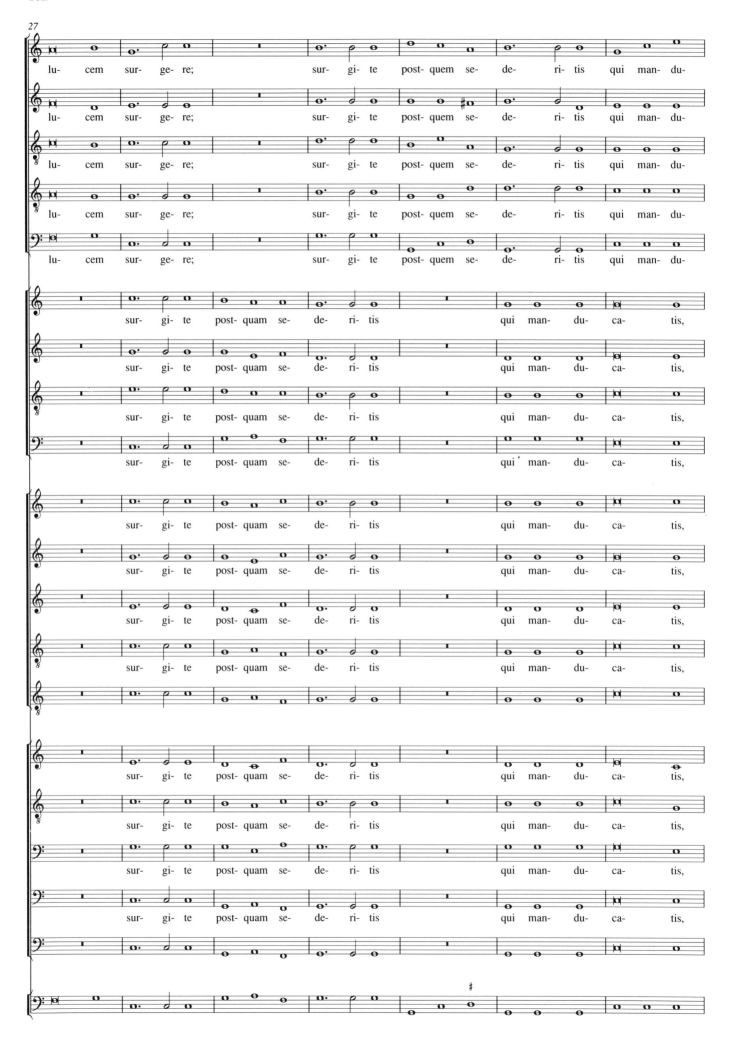

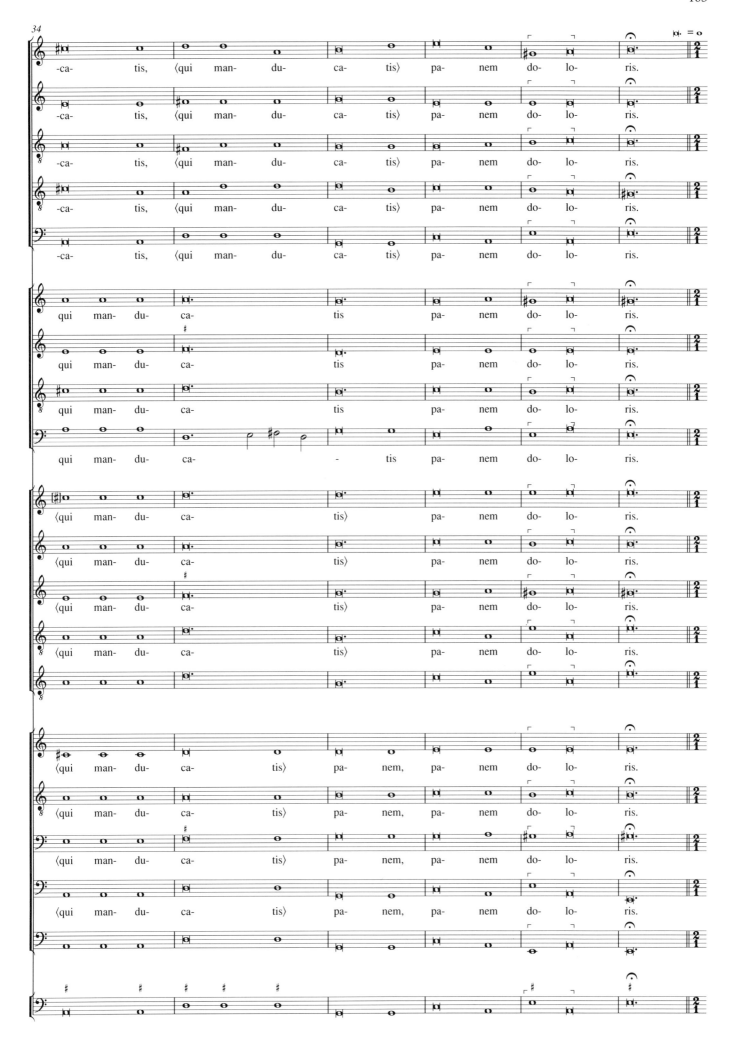

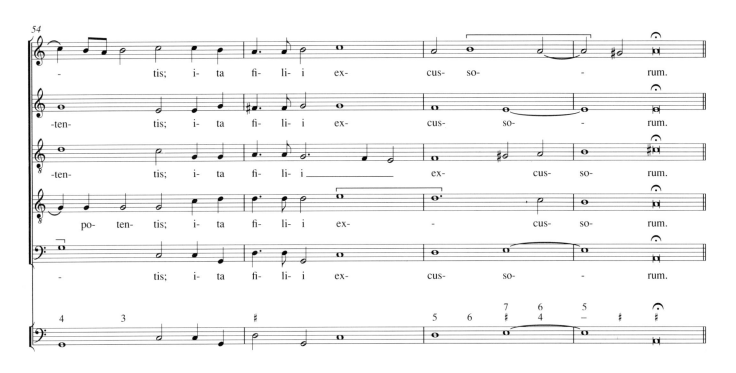

IX. Lauda Jerusalem (Psalm 147)

con-for-ta- vit se- ras por-ta- rum tu- a- rum; be-ne- di- xit, be-ne-di-xit fi- li-is tu- is in te. Qui

con-for-ta- vit se- ras por-ta- rum tu- a- rum; be-ne- di- xit, be-ne-di-xit fi- li-is tu- is in te. Qui

con-for-ta- vit se- ras por-ta- rum tu- a- rum, tu-a- rum; be-ne- di- xit, be-ne-di-xit fi- li- is tu- is in te. Qui

be-ne- di- xit, be-ne-di-xit fi- li-is tu- is in te. Qui

con-for-ta- vit se- ras por-ta- rum tu- a- rum; be-ne-di-xit fi- li-is tu- is in te. Qui

Qui

Qui

Qui

Qui

Qui

Qui

Qui

Qui

Qui

Qui

Qui

Qui

Qui

P.

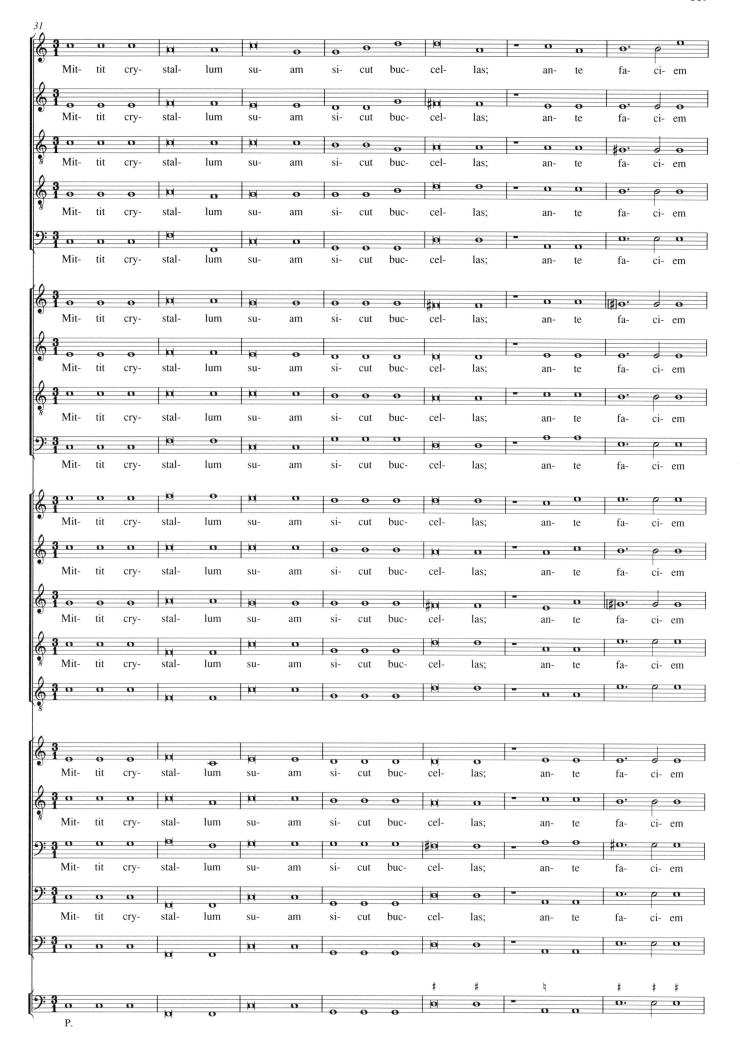

130

X. Magnificat

138

P.

148

152

XIa. Sinfonia a doi tenori

Subito Magnificat Sexti toni

XIb. Magnificat

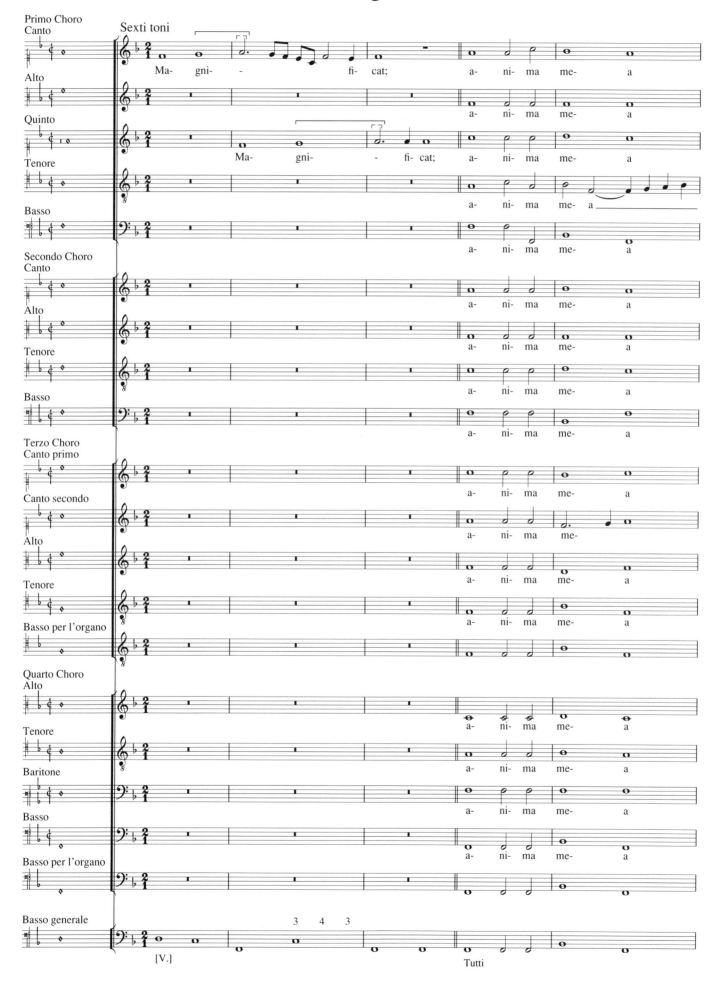

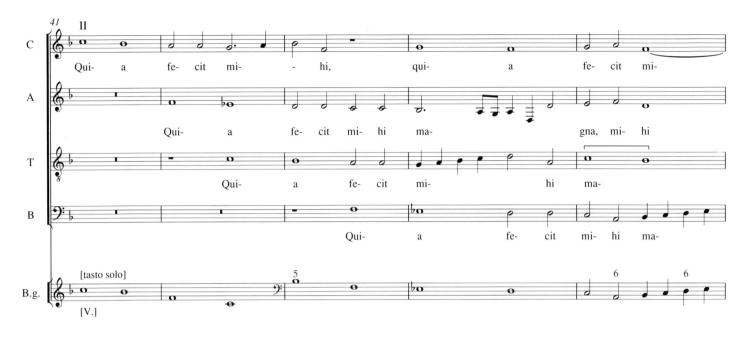

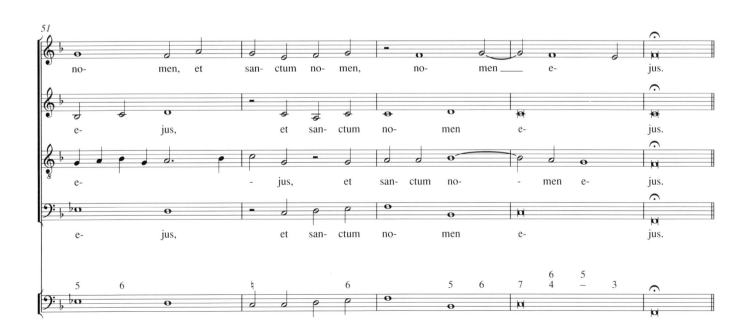

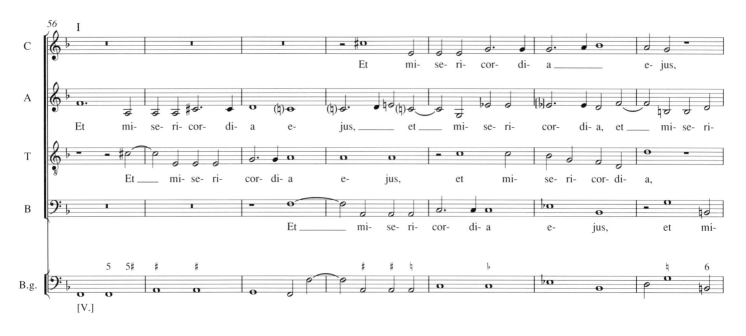

168

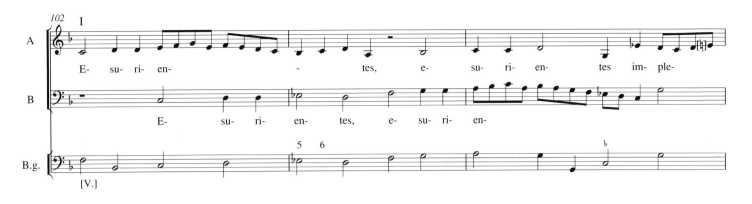

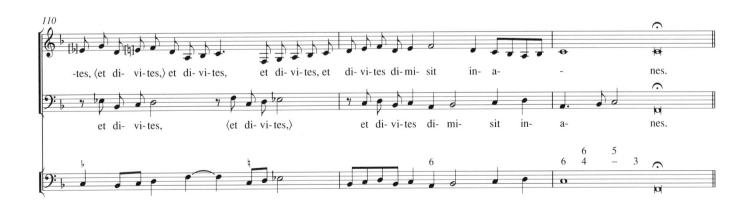

A 2. Basso solo è Soprano da nascosto.

Critical Report

Source

The only source is preserved in Bologna, Civico Museo Bibliografico Musicale (I-Bc), U.353. It consists of twenty partbooks: seventeen vocal partbooks, in quarto format; two organ bass books, in quarto format; and one general bass book, in folio format, which also contains the "Modo di concertare" on its final page. All twenty books have a "Tavola" (table of contents) after the music. The vocal partbooks are marked by the seventeen alphabetic letters from *A* through *R* (with *I* and *J* being identical), such that the recto folios in the canto partbook of Choir I are marked *A1*, *A2*, and so on. The alto and tenor partbooks of Choir I have their letters switched (so that the alto has *C* and the tenor has *B*). All pages in the partbooks for Choir II have printed the identifying term "Capella."

The frontispieces of the vocal partbooks read: SALMI | A QVATTRO | CHORI | Per cantare, e concertare nelle gran Solenni- | tà di tutto l'Anno, con il Basso continuo | per sonar nell'Organo | DI LODOVICO VIADANA | Maestro di Capella nel Domo di Fano. | OPERA XXVII. | Nouamente composta, & data in luce. | CON PRIVILE-GIO. | [printer's mark] | In Venetia, Appresso Giacomo Vincenti, 1612. In the frontispieces of the books for Choir III, "Ripieni del Terzo Choro Acuto si placet" is added. In those of Choir IV, "Ripieni del Quarto Choro Grave si placet" is added.

The frontispiece of the organ bass partbook of Choir III reads: BASSO PER L'ORGANO | ALL'OTTAVA ALTA | Del Terzo Choro Acuto | PER SONARE I SALMI . . . That of the organ bass book of Choir IV reads: BASSO PER L'ORGANO | ALL'OTTAVA BASSA | Del Quarto Choro Grave | PER SONARE I SALMI . . . That of the general bass book reads: BASSO | GENERALE | PER L'ORGANO | PER SONARE I SALMI . . .

Editorial Methods

The Music

The movement numbers, titles, and psalm numbers have been added; the mode numbers, however, are printed in the source at the beginning of each movement in all of the partbooks. The source uses Italian terms for the voices, choirs, and instruments, except in the case of the baritone voice of Choir IV, where the Latin "Baritonus" is used; in the edition, the original terms are retained except that the baritone is also given in Italian. The quinto part of Choir I, whose partbook follows that of the basso in the source, has been placed between the alto and tenor parts in the transcription since normally the quinto sings higher than the tenor, although it is not uncommon for these two voices to cross.

The original note values have been retained, except that longas for reciting tones have been transcribed as breves, and final longas (of both entire movements and sections within movements) have been transcribed as breves with added fermatas (with fermatas added over any resting parts as well). The unstemmed notes at the openings of movements II, VIII, and IX represent the *cantus planus* notation used for the introductory half-verses of the plainsong melodies, while in the *basso generale*, the note providing the pitch of the vocal entry has been transcribed as a quarter note with fermata. Source ligatures are marked by closed horizontal brackets above the notes, source coloration by open horizontal brackets. The tempo relationship between duple and triple sections is indicated by the equivalent note values added above the staff.

The source does have double barlines between sections, and these have been retained in the edition. The source also employs barlines before and after reciting tones, and each barline in the midst of the intonations at the beginnings of mvts. II and VIII is original. Barlines are also frequently used in the *basso generale* in order to clarify passages with quick notes and repeating leaps. Other barlines have been added as necessary, as have ties made necessary by the barlines. Source ties are reported in the critical notes to distinguish them from those added tacitly. Source slurs (all in mvt. V) have been removed and reported in the critical notes.

An incipit before each part shows the clef, key signature (if present), meter signature, any initial rests, and the initial note as found in the source. It should be noted that in mvts. III, V, X, and XIb, all parts not involved in the measured introductions (for one or two soloists with *basso generale*) begin—as their incipits show—after the introductions. In the transcription, the original C-clefs and the F-clef on the middle line (baritone clef) have been replaced by the modern G-clef (at pitch and transposed down an octave) and F-clef. The duple mensuration signs found in the source—¢ and C (with the latter's appearances so rare as to be viewed as mistakes)—have been modernized as ²⁄₂; the triple mensuration sign—**3**—has been modernized as ³⁄₁. In passages with reciting tones, the source usually has no mensuration signs and none have been added in the edition. In passages in duple meter, with the usual breve to a measure, isolated measures of a semibreve have also not been supplied with added mensuration signs (see, for example, mvt. III, m. 6).

The printer was rather careless with the exact placements of the *Pieno* and *Vuoto* indications, either written out (with *Vuoto* spelled as *Voto*) or abbreviated. In the edition the placements of these indications are adjusted as necessary according to the given contexts and are always abbreviated (as P. and V.). Editorially added abbreviations are placed in brackets. The many indications of voicing and instrumentation found in the *basso generale* partbook (and to a lesser extent in the other partbooks as well) are not included in the edition where they have been made redundant by placing the music in score. However, the "Tutti" indications in the *basso generale* have been retained.

Tasto solo indications have been added in brackets where called for by Viadana's rule five of the *Cento concerti ecclesiastici:* "When a concerto begins after the manner of a fugue, the organist begins also with a single note, and, on the entry of several parts, it is at his discretion to accompany them as he pleases."

The notation of accidentals has been regularized to conform with modern practice. Source accidentals made redundant by the addition of barlines have been tacitly removed. Since only sharps and flats are used in the source (both in the parts and in the figured basses), these have been tacitly replaced by natural signs where called for by modern conventions. Sharp signs in the source meant to indicate that *una nota super la* should not be flatted (as found in mvt. I, quinto of Choir I, m. 16, note 3, for example) have been tacitly removed. Editorial accidentals are placed in brackets on the staff, while added cautionary accidentals are placed in parentheses on the staff. Accidentals placed above the staff are meant to indicate the proper uses of *musica ficta*.

As noted in the Introduction, Viadana only uses accidentals in the figured basses of the two *basso per l'organo* parts and the *basso generale*. In this edition, however, a complete editorial figured bass is provided, including figures, above the *basso generale* staff. In order to make it possible to "reconstruct" the original figured-bass accidentals, the reader will find these reported in the critical notes.

The Texts

Archaic spellings in the Vulgate text have been modernized, such that "Ierusalem" or "Hierusalem" is spelled as "Jerusalem," and "vtero" is spelled as "utero." Abbreviations are tacitly spelled out (for instance, the ampersand is given as "et," while "scabellū" is given as "scabellum"). Text repetitions indicated in the source by *ij* or *ii* are presented in full in the transcription within angle brackets. The beginning of each psalm verse is capitalized, as are names (Jacob, Israel) and references to the divinity (Deus, Spiritui Sancto).

As is well known, nearly every psalm verse falls into two halves, and these are articulated in Gregorian recitation with intonations leading to the *mediatio* and *terminatio* respectively. Occasionally there are psalm verses of such length that a strict application of this general method would lead to an overly protracted recitation. For these, the first half of the verse is subdivided by a small inflection, the flex.

The punctuation of the text underlay in the source is inconsistent and so does not reflect the structure of the psalm verses. However, Viadana does take that structure into account in his settings, and therefore, the punctuation of the psalm verses in the edition has been regularized as follows: (1) a semicolon divides the two halves of a psalm verse, unless the second half is a declamatory text that might be read as though between quotation marks, in which case a colon is used with the first word of the second half being capitalized (as in the beginning of Psalm 109: Dixit Dominus Domino meo: Sede a dextris meis [The Lord said unto my Lord: "Sit thou at my right hand"]), and (2) a comma is used to indicate a flex.

There are frequent repetitions of words, phrases, and half-verses in the score, and these have been set off by commas in the edition. It is remarkable that at one point Viadana repeats a complete verse, the sixth of Psalm 111 (see mm. 50–62, where the initial statement of the verse ends with a half cadence in m. 54 before its repetition).

Critical Notes

The voices and instruments are abbreviated as follows: ChI, II, III, IV = Choir I, II, III, IV; C = Canto; C1 = Canto primo; C2 = Canto secondo; A = Alto; Q = Quinto; T = Tenore; Bar. = Baritone; B = Basso; B.p.o. = Basso per l'organo; B.g. = Basso generale. However, in the reports of the figured-bass accidentals, where only the two Basso per l'organo parts are involved, they are identified as "both B.p.o.'s," and where the Basso generale is added to these, the identification is "all three bassos." The values of notes in the source in relation to those in the edition are as follows: longa = double whole note with or without a fermata (see "Editorial Methods"); breve = double whole note; semibreve = whole note; minim = half note; semiminim = quarter note; fusa = eighth note; semifusa = sixteenth note. Pitches are designated according to the system in which middle C = c'. The reports for each movement begin with a paragraph specifically devoted to those of the figured-bass accidentals.

I. Deus in adjutorium

Figure is ♯ at m. 6, ChIV/B.p.o. and B.g., note 1; m. 8, ChIV/B.p.o. and B.g., notes 2 and 3; mm. 22, 23, and 25, all three bassos, note 1; m. 29, ChIII/B.p.o., note 2; and m. 29, B.g., notes 1 and 2.

II. Dixit Dominus

Figure is ♭ at m. 8, B.g., note 1; m. 30, all three bassos, note 2; m. 92, ChIV/B.p.o. and B.g., note 2; m. 95, B.g., note 1; and m. 96, ChIV/B.p.o. and B.g., note 1. Figure is ♯ at m. 8, B.g., note 2; m. 14, B.g., notes 1 and 3; m. 15, B.g., note 1; m. 18, B.g., note 7; m. 19, both B.p.o.'s, note 1; m. 19, B.g., note 2; m. 20, all three bassos, notes 1 and 2; m. 27, both B.p.o.'s, notes 3 and 4; m. 27, B.g., note 2; m. 28, ChIII/B.p.o., notes 1 and 2; m. 28, ChIV/B.p.o., notes 1, 2, 3, and 4; m. 28, B.g., note 1; m. 31, both B.p.o.'s, note 1; m. 31, B.g., notes 1 and 2; m. 32, all three bassos, note 1; m. 40, both B.p.o.'s, note 4; m. 40, B.g., note 3; m. 43, ChIII/B.p.o., notes 1 and 3; m. 43, ChIV/B.p.o. and B.g., notes 1 and 2; m. 56, both B.p.o.'s, note 1; m. 56, B.g., notes 1 and 2; m. 57, all three bassos, note 1; m. 60, ChIII/B.p.o. and B.g., note 2; m. 60, ChIV/B.p.o., note 3; m. 61, ChIII/B.p.o., note 1; m. 71, B.g., note 3; m. 77, all three bassos, note 2; m. 78, ChIII/B.p.o. and B.g., note 1; m. 82, ChIV/B.p.o., notes 1 and 2; m. 84, B.g., note 6; m. 85, ChIII/B.p.o. and B.g., notes 4 and 5; m. 85, ChIV/B.p.o., note 4; m. 89, all three bassos, note 1; m. 93, all three bassos, note 1; m. 94, ChIV/B.p.o., notes 1, 2, and 3; and m. 97, all three bassos, note 1.

M. 6, ChI/A, note 3 is f'; ChI/T, note 3 is c'. M. 22, ChII/T, note 2 is d'. Mm. 24–25, ChIII/B.p.o., tie is original. M. 26, ChII/C, note 3 is b♯'. M. 27, ChII/C, note 1 is c''. M. 37, B.g., note 3 is minim, note 4 is lacking. Mm. 59–60, ChII/T, notes 4–6 (of m. 59) are lacking, syllables "-i-nas" fall under m. 60, notes 1–2, and "implebit" (mm. 59–60) is lacking. M. 85, B.g., note 2 is A. M. 91, ChIV/A, note 2 is e[♭]'.

III. Confitebor tibi

Figure is ♯ at m. 10, ChIV/B.p.o. and B.g., note 3; m. 20, B.g., note 1; m. 26, B.g., note 8; m. 29, B.g., note 3; m. 33, all three bassos, note 3; m. 34, ChIV/B.p.o., note 1; m. 34, B.g., notes 1, 2, and 3; m. 37, ChIII/B.p.o., note 1; m. 37, ChIV/B.p.o., notes 1 and 3; m. 37, B.g., note 2; m. 42, all three bassos, note 1; m. 43, B.g., note 3; m. 44, B.g., note 1; m. 47, B.g., notes 3 and 6; m. 48, B.g., notes 4 and 5; m. 49, B.g., notes 3 and 4; m. 50, B.g., note 4; m. 51, B.g., notes 3 and 4; m. 52, B.g., note 3; m. 54, B.g., note 1; m. 60, B.g., note 3; m. 61, B.g., notes 4 and 5; m. 62, B.g., note 1; m. 64, B.g., note 1; m. 68, all three bassos, note 1; m. 74, all three bassos, note 1; m. 80, B.g., notes 1 and 2; m. 89, B.g., note 1; m. 92, B.g., note 6; m. 93, B.g., notes 3 and 5; m. 95, all three bassos, note 3; m. 101, ChIV/B.p.o. and B.g., notes 1 and 2; m. 107, B.g., note 4; m. 114, B.g., note 2; m. 124, ChIII/B.p.o. and B.g., note 5; m. 127, ChIV/B.p.o., note 3; m. 127, B.g., note 2.

Mm. 40–41, B.g., tie is original.   Mm. 59–60, B.g., tie is original.   M. 61, B.g., note 1 is d.   M. 69, ChII/A, note 5 is d'.   Mm. 79–80, ChI/B, tie is original.   Mm. 90–91 and 91–92, ChIII/B.p.o., tie is original. M. 100, ChIII/B.p.o., note 1 is two tied minims separated by barline.   Mm. 116–17, ChI/C, text is "Gloria Patri."   M. 129, ChII/C, syllables "-men" and "a-" are lacking.

IV. Beatus vir

Figure is ♯ at m. 9, ChIV/B.p.o., note 3; m. 17, B.g., notes 2 and 4; m. 26, B.g., note 3; m. 28, B.g., note 2; m. 32, B.g., notes 1 and 3; m. 39, B.g., note 1; m. 66, both B.p.o.'s, note 2; m. 91, B.g., notes 2 and 4; m. 92, B.g., note 2; m. 101, B.g., note 4; m. 109, ChIII/B.p.o., note 1; m. 109, ChIV/B.p.o. and B.g., note 2; m. 111, all three bassos, note 3; m. 112, ChIV/B.p.o., note 1; m. 116, B.g., note 2; m. 117, B.g., note 6; m. 120, all three bassos, note 3.

M. 61, B.g., note 4 is fusa.   M. 69, ChII/T, notes 3–4 are a.   M. 120, ChI/T, note 1 is a; ChI/B, note 1 is A; B.g., note 1 is A.   M. 122, ChII/A, note 1 is e'.   M. 122, ChI/C, note 3 is semibreve, notes 4–5 have been added to fill the interval to m. 123, note 1.

V. Laudate pueri

Figure is ♭ at m. 17, ChIV/B.p.o. and B.g., note 2; m. 37, B.g., note 3; m. 53, B.g., note 2; m. 56, B.g., note 1; m. 87, B.g., note 1; m. 103, ChIV/B.p.o., note 2; and m. 104, ChIV/B.p.o. and B.g., note 2. Figure is ♯ at m. 9, B.g., note 4; m. 11, ChIV/B.p.o. and B.g., note 1; m. 13, ChIV/B.p.o. and B.g., note 2; m. 14, ChIV/B.p.o. and B.g., note 1; m. 17, ChIV/B.p.o. and B.g., note 4; m. 18, ChIV/B.p.o. and B.g., note 1; m. 24, B.g., note 5; m. 27, B.g., note 5; m. 29, B.g., note 1; m. 39, ChIV/B.p.o. and B.g., note 1; m. 41, ChIV/B.p.o., notes 2 and 3; m. 41, B.g., note 2; m. 42, ChIV/B.p.o., note 1; m. 42, B.g., notes 1 and 2; m. 43, B.g., note 1; m. 44, B.g., notes 4, 6, and 8; m. 48, B.g., note 1; m. 49, B.g., note 3; m. 53, ChIV/B.p.o. and B.g., note 3; m. 54, ChIV/B.p.o. and B.g., note 1; m. 55, B.g., notes 1, 2, 3, and 4; m. 62, B.g., notes 1 and 2; m. 65, B.g., note 5; m. 71, both B.p.o.'s, note 3; m. 71, B.g., notes 1 and 4; m. 73, both B.p.o.'s, note 2; m. 73, B.g., notes 1 and 3; m. 77, both B.p.o.'s, note 1; m. 77, B.g., note 6; m. 78, ChIII/B.p.o., notes 3 and 4; m. 78, ChIV/B.p.o., note 4; m. 78, B.g., note 1; m. 79, both B.p.o.'s, note 2; m. 79, B.g., note 1; m. 80, both B.p.o.'s, note 2; m. 82, B.g., note 4; m. 83, both B.p.o.'s, note 2; m. 84, both B.p.o.'s, note 2; m. 84, B.g., notes 1 and 3; m. 85, ChIV/B.p.o., note 2; m. 85, B.g., notes 1 and 3; m. 91, B.g., note 4; m. 93, ChIV/B.p.o. and B.g., note 1; m. 95, ChIV/B.p.o. and B.g., note 2; m. 96, all three bassos, note 1; m. 99, all three bassos, note 3; m. 100, ChIV/B.p.o., note 1; m. 103, all three bassos, note 3; m. 104, all three bassos, note 1; and m. 105, all three bassos, note 1.

M. 1, note 2, to m. 2, note 1, ChI/C has slur.   M. 2, note 2, to m. 3, note 1, ChI/Q has slur.   M. 4, ChI/C, rest is lacking.   Mm. 21–22, B.g., tie is original.   M. 58, B.g., notes 3–4 are c, G.   M. 59, ChI/Q, slur on notes 1–2.   M. 83, ChII/A, note 1 has ♯.   M. 103, ChI/A, note 1 has ♯; ChII/A, note 1 has ♯.

VI. Laudate Dominum

Figure is ♭ at m. 72, B.g., note 3; and m. 74, B.g., note 3. Figure is ♯ at m. 1, B.g., note 3; m. 2, both B.p.o.'s, notes 1, 2, and 3; m. 2, B.g., note 3; m. 3, ChIII/B.p.o., notes 1 and 3; m. 3, ChIV/B.p.o., notes 2 and 3; m. 3, B.g., notes 1, 2, and 3; m. 10, B.g., notes 1, 2, and 3; m. 13, all three bassos, notes 1, 2, and 3; m. 25, both B.p.o.'s, notes 1 and 2; m. 25, B.g., notes 1, 2, and 3; m. 26, B.g., notes 1 and 2; m. 27, B.g., notes 1 and 2; m. 28, both B.p.o.'s, note 2; m. 28, B.g., notes 1 and 2; m. 31, all three bassos, note 2; m. 33, B.g., note 2; m. 35, all three bassos, note 2; m. 36, both B.p.o.'s, notes 1 and 2; m. 37, both B.p.o.'s note 2; m. 40, all three bassos, note 2; m. 41, ChIV/B.p.o., note 1; m. 42, B.g., notes 1, 2, and 3; m. 55, B.g., note 1; m. 57, all three bassos, note 1; m. 59, both B.p.o.'s note 1; m. 65, all three bassos, note 2; m. 66, B.g., note 2; m. 69, all three bassos, note 2; m. 70, both B.p.o.'s, notes 1 and 2; m. 70, B.g., note 2; m. 73, both B.p.o.'s, note 2; and m. 77, all three bassos, note 1.

M. 14, ChI/B, figured-bass ♯ above note 2. M. 19, ChIV/T, note 3 is a. M. 24, ChIII/A, notes 1–3 are semibreves. M. 34, ChI/T, note has ♯. M. 45, ChI/Q, note has ♯.

VII. Laetatus sum

Figure is ♭ at m. 92, B.g., note 1. Figure is ♯ at m. 8, B.g., note 3; m. 9, B.g., notes 2, 3, and 6; m. 16, B.g., note 2; m. 20, B.g., note 1; m. 23, B.g., note 5; m. 29, B.g., note 3; m. 39, B.g., note 5; m. 54, both B.p.o.'s, note 1; m. 54, B.g., notes 1 and 2; m. 63, B.g., note 1; m. 72, B.g., note 3; m. 74, B.g., notes 5 and 6; m. 75, B.g., note 1; m. 82, B.g., note 1; m. 89, B.g., note 1; m. 92, B.g., note 2; m. 94, B.g., notes 1 and 2; m. 98, B.g., notes 4 and 6; m. 99, B.g., note 6; m. 114, B.g., note 2; m. 115, B.g., notes 1, 2, and 3; m. 116, B.g., notes 1 and 2; m. 123, all three bassos, note 3; and m. 124, B.g., note 1.

M. 6, ChII/B, semibreve rest is lacking. M. 9, B.g., tie is original. M. 53, ChIV/B.p.o., note 2 is F. M. 66, ChI/Q, note 3 is a. M. 75, ChI/A, note 4 is e′; ChII/A, notes 4 and 6 are e′; ChIII/C1, note 5 is c″. Mm. 83–85, ChII/A, notes match those of ChI/A. M. 86, ChI/A, tie is original; ChI/T, tie is original. M. 87, ChI/Q, tie is original; ChI/B, tie is original. M. 100, B.g., notes 3–4, tie is original. Mm. 100–101, B.g., tie is original.

VIII. Nisi Dominus

Figure is ♭ at m. 16, B.g., note 3. Figure is ♯ at m. 3, B.g., notes 1 and 3; m. 4, ChIII/B.p.o., notes 1 and 3; m. 4, ChIV/B.p.o., note 1; m. 4, B.g., notes 1, 3, and 4; m. 10, ChIII/B.p.o. and B.g., note 1; m. 11, B.g., notes 1, 3, and 4; m. 12, B.g., notes 1 and 2; m. 15, B.g., note 1; m. 19, B.g., notes 2 and 4; m. 20, B.g., notes 1 and 2; m. 21, ChIII/B.p.o. note 2; m. 21, ChIV/B.p.o. and B.g., notes 1 and 2; m. 22, ChIII/B.p.o., note 2; m. 22, ChIV/B.p.o. and B.g., notes 1 and 2; m. 23, ChIII/B.p.o., note 2; m. 23, ChIV/B.p.o. and B.g., notes 1 and 2; m. 31, B.g., note 3; m. 34, both B.p.o.'s, notes 1, 2, and 3; m. 34, B.g., notes 1 and 2; m. 35, B.g., notes 1, 2, and 3; m. 38, all three bassos, note 1; m. 39, all three bassos, note

1; m. 43, B.g., note 4; m. 49, B.g., note 6; m. 50, B.g., note 2; m. 56, B.g., note 2; m. 57, B.g., note 2; m. 58, B.g., note 1; m. 59, B.g., notes 1 and 2; m. 60, B.g., notes 1 and 2; m. 61, B.g., note 1; m. 65, both B.p.o.'s note 1; m. 68, B.g., note 6; m. 70, ChIII/B.p.o. and B.g., note 1; m. 71, ChIII/B.p.o., note 1; m. 71, B.g., notes 3, 4, 5, and 6; m. 72, ChIII/B.p.o., note 2; m. 74, all three bassos, note 1; m. 75, B.g., notes 2 and 5; m. 85, ChIII/B.p.o., note 1; m. 86, ChIV/B.p.o. and B.g., note 1; m. 91, all three bassos, note 3; m. 92, ChIII/B.p.o. and B.g., notes 1, 2, and 3; m. 93, ChIV/B.p.o. and B.g., note 4; and m. 95, ChIII/B.p.o. and B.g., note 1.

M. 2, ChI/T, note 8 is longa. M. 10, ChIV/B.p.o., note is d. M. 14, B.g., note 4 is two tied semiminims separated by barline. M. 15, ChI/T, syllable "e-" falls under note 2. Mm. 17–18, B.g., tie is original. M. 42, ChI/C, note 8 is semifusa. M. 59, ChI/C, note 2 is g[♯]′. M. 60, ChII/A, note 2 is d′. M. 68, B.g., tie is original. M. 77, ChI/B, tie is original. M. 91, ChII/T, note 2 is g. M. 92, ChI/Q, note 1 is semibreve, rest is minim rest; ChIV/A, notes 2–3 are c♯′. M. 94, ChIII/ C2, note 5 has ♯. M. 95, ChIII/T, note is a.

IX. Lauda Jerusalem

Figure is ♯ at m. 3, all three bassos, note 3; m. 6, B.g., note 1; m. 14, B.g., notes 1 and 2; m. 15, both B.p.o.'s, notes 1, 2, 3, 4, and 5; m. 15, B.g., notes 1, 2, 3, 4, 5, and 6; m. 16, ChIII/B.p.o., notes 1 and 2; m. 16, ChIV/B.p.o. and B.g., notes 1, 2, and 3; m. 20, B.g., note 6; m. 21, B.g., note 6; m. 23, all three bassos, note 3; m. 35, B.g., notes 1 and 2; m. 36, ChIII/B.p.o., notes 1 and 2; m. 37, all three bassos, notes 1, 2, and 3; m. 38, ChIII/B.p.o. and B.g., notes 1, 2, and 3; m. 38, ChIV/B.p.o., notes 2 and 3; m. 41, ChIII/B.p.o. and B.g., note 1; m. 43, B.g., note 4; m. 52, ChIV/B.p.o. and B.g., note 2; m. 63, ChIV/B.p.o., note 3; m. 63, B.g., note 2; m. 64, B.g., note 1; m. 70, both B.p.o.'s, note 1; m. 70, B.g., note 2; and m. 78, all three bassos, note 1.

M. 5, ChI/A, note 9 is semiminim. M. 10, ChI/T, note 7 is c′; B.g., note 4 is minim c, note 5 has been added. M. 12, ChI/A, syllable "-ti" falls under note 7. Mm. 9–15, ChIII/A, pattern of rests is three semibreves too long. Mm. 24–30, ChIII/A, pattern of rests is two breves too short. Mm. 52–57, ChIII/B.p.o., pattern of rests is one semibreve too short. M. 59, ChIV/A, note 1 has ♯. M. 60, ChI/A, note 2 is semiminim. M. 61, ChI/T, note 3 is semibreve g, which extends through m. 62, note 1.

X. Magnificat

Figure is ♭ at m. 4, B.g., note 1; m. 63, B.g., note 3; m. 85, B.g., note 1; m. 87, B.g., note 3; m. 107, B.g., note 1; m. 114, B.g., note 2; m. 115, B.g., note 1; and m. 118, ChIII/B.p.o. and B.g., note 1. Figure is ♯ at m. 3, ChIII/B.p.o., notes 1, 2, and 3; m. 3, B.g., notes 1 and 2; m. 4, B.g., note 2; m. 5, B.g., note 1; m. 6, ChIII/B.p.o., note 3; m. 6, B.g., note 2; m. 7, ChIII/B.p.o. and B.g., note 1; m. 9, B.g., note 2; m. 10, ChIII/B.p.o., note 2; m. 10, B.g., notes 1 and 2; m. 16, B.g., note 4; m. 18, B.g., note 1; m. 20, B.g., note 3; m. 23, ChIII/B.p.o. and B.g., note 2; m. 29, B.g., notes 4 and 6; m. 30, B.g., notes 2 and 3; m. 31, B.g., notes 2 and 3; m. 38,

B.g., note 2; m. 39, B.g., note 3; m. 41, ChIII/B.p.o., note 1; m. 41, B.g., notes 1 and 2; m. 42, B.g., note 1; m. 43, B.g., note 2; m. 45, B.g., notes 1 and 2; m. 46, B.g., note 1; m. 48, B.g., notes 1 and 3; m. 55, ChIII/B.p.o. note 1; m. 59, B.g., note 1; m. 60, B.g., note 2; m. 61, B.g., note 2; m. 63, ChIII/B.p.o., note 2; m. 64, ChIII/B.p.o. and B.g., note 1; m. 69, B.g., note 1; m. 75, ChIII/B.p.o., note 3; m. 75, B.g., note 2; m. 80, B.g., notes 1 and 3; m. 86, B.g., notes 1 and 3; m. 87, B.g., notes 1 and 2; m. 88, ChIII/B.p.o. and B.g., note 3; m. 89, B.g., note 1; m. 91, B.g., note 5; m. 94, B.g., note 4; m. 97, B.g., note 4; m. 98, B.g., note 1; m. 102, all three bassos, note 1; m. 106, B.g., notes 1 and 2; m. 107, ChIII/B.p.o. and B.g., note 3; m. 111, B.g., note 7; m. 112, B.g., notes 5 and 6; m. 115, ChIII/B.p.o., note 3; m. 115, B.g., note 2; m. 116, B.g., notes 1 and 2; m. 117, ChIII/B.p.o. and B.g., note 4; and m. 119, B.g., note 1.

M. 18, ChIII/C2, semibreve rest is lacking. Mm. 31–32, B.g., tie is original. M. 40, ChII/T, note 1 is dotted semibreve and note 2 is lacking. M. 43, B.g., note 3 is two tied semiminims separated by barline. M. 48, ChIII/C2, minim rest is lacking. Mm. 48–49, B.g., tie is original. Mm. 71–72, ChII/C, text is "implevit bonis," which is repeated in mm. 73–74 using *ij.* M. 74, B.g., note 2 is lacking. M. 103, ChIV/Bar., semibreve rest is lacking. M. 116, ChII/A, note 1 is d', notes 2–3 are f'. M. 116, ChII/T, note 2 is semibreve a, which extends through m. 117, note 1. M. 117, ChII/A, note 1 is f'; ChII/T, note 2 is a.

XIa. Sinfonia a doi tenori

Figure is ♯ at m. 8, B.g., note 1; m. 9, B.g., notes 4 and 6; m. 11, B.g., notes 3 and 5; m. 12, B.g., notes 2 and 4; m. 13, B.g., note 4; and m. 45, B.g., note 2.

M. 23, B.g., note 2 is semibreve, rest is lacking.

XIb. Magnificat

Figure is ♭ at m. 50, B.g., note 1; m. 82, B.g., note 4; m. 94, B.g., note 4; m. 115, B.g., note 3; m. 124, B.g., note 4; m. 129, B.g., note 2; and m. 133, B.g., note 4. Figure is ♯ at m. 6, ChIII/B.p.o. and B.g., note 2; m. 15, B.g., note 1; m. 26, B.g., note 4; m. 27, B.g., notes 1 and 2; m. 29, B.g., note 2; m. 35, ChIII/B.p.o., notes 1 and 2; m. 35, B.g., note 2; m. 36, ChIII/B.p.o., notes 1, 2, and 4; m. 36, B.g., notes 1 and 2; m. 57, B.g., notes 1 and 2; m. 65, B.g., note 2; m. 77, B.g., note 3; m. 78, all three bassos, note 1; m. 80, ChIII/B.p.o. and B.g., note 4; m. 80, ChIV/B.p.o., notes 4 and 5; m. 83, ChIII/B.p.o., note 2; m. 83, B.g., notes 2 and 3; m. 85, both B.p.o.'s, note 3; m. 85, B.g., note 1; m. 94, B.g., note 3; m. 99, B.g., notes 1 and 3; m. 100, all three bassos, notes 1 and 2; m. 101, all three bassos, note 1; m. 109, B.g., note 2; m. 116, B.g., note 1; m. 145, ChIII/B.p.o., note 3; and m. 145, ChIV/B.p.o. and B.g., notes 3 and 4.

M. 16, ChI/C, syllable "-o" is lacking. M. 35, ChI/T, note 4 is a; ChIII/A, notes 3–6 are g'. Between m. 36 and m. 37, ChIII/C1, source has:

Mm. 56–57, ChI/T, tie is original. Mm. 58–59, B.g., tie is original. M. 72, ChI/T, note 2 is c'. M. 80, ChI/A, note 2 is d'. M. 86, B.g., note 3 is semiminim. Mm. 86–87 and 87–88, B.g., tie is original. Mm. 87–88, ChIV/A, text is "mente cordis." M. 110, B.g., tie is original. M. 116, ChI/Q, note 1 is minim. M. 128, B.g., note 2 is f. M. 133, ChI/B, notes 11–12 are semiminims. M. 134, ChI/B, tie is original. M. 134, B.g., note 1 is minim, note 2 is lacking. M. 135, ChI/B, tie is original.

RECENT RESEARCHES IN THE MUSIC OF THE BAROQUE ERA
Christoph Wolff, general editor

Vol.   *Composer: Title*

1   Marc-Antoine Charpentier: *Judicium Salomonis*

2   Georg Philipp Telemann: *Forty-eight Chorale Preludes*

3   Johann Caspar Kerll: *Missa Superba*

4–5   Jean-Marie Leclair: *Sonatas for Violin and Basso Continuo, Opus 5*

6   *Ten Eighteenth-Century Voluntaries*

7–8   William Boyce: *Two Anthems for the Georgian Court*

9   Giulio Caccini: *Le Nuove musiche*

10–11   Jean-Marie Leclair: *Sonatas for Violin and Basso Continuo, Opus 9 and Opus 15*

12   Johann Ernst Eberlin: *Te Deum, Dixit Dominus, Magnificat*

13   Gregor Aichinger: *Cantiones Ecclesiasticae*

14–15   Giovanni Legrenzi: *Cantatas and Canzonets for Solo Voice*

16   Giovanni Francesco Anerio and Francesco Soriano: *Two Settings of Palestrina's Missa Papae Marcelli*

17   Giovanni Paolo Colonna: *Messe a nove voci concertata con stromenti*

18   Michel Corrette: *Premier livre d'orgue and Nouveau livre de noels*

19   Maurice Greene: *Voluntaries and Suites for Organ and Harpsichord*

20   Giovanni Antonio Piani: *Sonatas for Violin Solo and Violoncello with Cembalo*

21–22   Marin Marais: *Six Suites for Viol and Thoroughbass*

23–24   Dario Castello: *Selected Ensemble Sonatas*

25   *A Neapolitan Festa a Ballo and Selected Instrumental Ensemble Pieces*

26   Antonio Vivaldi: *The Manchester Violin Sonatas*

27   Louis-Nicolas Clérambault: *Two Cantatas for Soprano and Chamber Ensemble*

28   Giulio Caccini: *Nuove musiche e nuova maniera di scriverle (1614)*

29–30   Michel Pignolet de Montéclair: *Cantatas for One and Two Voices*

31   Tomaso Albinoni: *Twelve Cantatas, Opus 4*

32–33   Antonio Vivaldi: *Cantatas for Solo Voice*

34   Johann Kuhnau: *Magnificat*

35   Johann Stadlmayr: *Selected Magnificats*

36–37   Jacopo Peri: *Euridice: An Opera in One Act, Five Scenes*

38   Francesco Severi: *Salmi passaggiati (1615)*

39   George Frideric Handel: *Six Concertos for the Harpsichord or Organ (Walsh's Transcriptions, 1738)*

40   *The Brasov Tablature: German Keyboard Studies, 1608–1684*

41   John Coprario: *Twelve Fantasias for Two Bass Viols and Organ and Eleven Pieces for Three Lyra Viols*

42   Antonio Cesti: *Il Pomo d'oro: Music for Acts III and V from Modena, Biblioteca Estense, Ms. Mus. E. 120*

43   Tomaso Albinoni: *Pimpinone: Intermezzi comici musicali*

44–45   Antonio Lotti: *Duetti, terzetti, e madrigali a più voci*

46   Matthias Weckmann: *Four Sacred Concertos*

47   Jean Gilles: *Requiem (Messe des morts)*

48   Marc-Antoine Charpentier: *Vocal Chamber Music*

49   *Spanish Art Song in the Seventeenth Century*

50   Jacopo Peri: *Le Varie musiche and Other Songs*

51–52   Tomaso Albinoni: *Sonatas and Suites, Opus 8, for Two Violins, Violoncello, and Basso Continuo*

53   Agostino Steffani: *Twelve Chamber Duets*

54–55   Gregor Aichinger: *The Vocal Concertos*

56   Giovanni Battista Draghi: *Harpsichord Music*

57   *Concerted Sacred Music of the Bologna School*

58   Jean-Marie Leclair: *Sonatas for Violin and Basso Continuo, Opus 2*

59   Isabella Leonarda: *Selected Compositions*

60–61   Johann Schelle: *Six Chorale Cantatas*

62   Denis Gaultier: *La Rhétorique des Dieux*

63   Marc-Antoine Charpentier: *Music for Molière's Comedies*

64–65   Georg Philipp Telemann: *Don Quichotte auf der Hochzeit des Comacho: Comic Opera-Serenata in One Act*

66   Henry Butler: *Collected Works*

67–68   John Jenkins: *The Lyra Viol Consorts*

69   *Keyboard Transcriptions from the Bach Circle*

70   Melchior Franck: *Geistliche Gesäng und Melodeyen*

71   Georg Philipp Telemann: *Douze solos, à violon ou traversière*

72   Marc-Antoine Charpentier: *Nine Settings of the Litanies de la Vierge*

73   *The Motets of Jacob Praetorius II*

74   Giovanni Porta: *Selected Sacred Music from the Ospedale della Pietà*

75   *Fourteen Motets from the Court of Ferdinand II of Hapsburg*

76   Jean-Marie Leclair: *Sonatas for Violin and Basso Continuo, Opus 1*

77   Antonio Bononcini: *Complete Sonatas for Violoncello and Basso Continuo*

78   Christoph Graupner: *Concerti Grossi for Two Violins*

79   Paolo Quagliati: *Libro primo de' madrigali a quattro voci*

80   Melchior Franck: *Dulces Mundani Exilij Deliciae*

81   *Late-Seventeenth-Century English Keyboard Music*

82   *Solo Compositions for Violin and Viola da gamba with Basso Continuo*

83   Barbara Strozzi: *Cantate, ariete a una, due e tre voci, Opus 3*

84   Charles-Hubert Gervais: *Super flumina Babilonis*

85   Henry Aldrich: *Selected Anthems and Motet Recompositions*

86   Lodovico Grossi da Viadana: *Salmi a quattro cori*